Faith Elicia

Do You See What I See?

Copyright

Do You See What I See?

Copyright © 2021 by Faith Elicia

All rights reserved. This copy is intended for the original purchaser of this book ONLY. No part of this book may be reproduced, scanned, or distributed in any printed or electronic form without prior written permission from Faith Elicia. Please do not participate in or encourage piracy of copyrighted materials in violation of the author's rights. Purchase only authorized editions.

Image/art disclaimer: Licensed material is being used for illustrative purposes only. Any person or character depicted in the licensed material is a model.

Paperback ISBN: 978-1-948989-20-6

Editor: Faith Elicia
Cover Artist and Illustrator: Faith Elicia
Photography: Suzanne Cosme
Interior Layout and Cover Design: www.sceneticdesigns.com

Published in the United States of America

Dedication

To Mom and Dad
For raising me with love in your heart
And filling me with my own

Foreword

Benaaz Russell, PsyD, CEDS

"No Whac-A-Mole!"

I often find myself saying this to clients recovering from eating disorders.

Whac-A-Mole is an arcade game that involves bopping little moles on the head as they pop up. Speed is necessary to hit them.

Recovery from an eating disorder can be similar in that things are always popping up that clients have to deal with. These situations can be frustrating, create havoc, spark anger and a defeatist attitude. However, they can also create growth opportunities, challenging oneself to act differently and view situations through different lenses.

When it comes to recovery, speed isn't a requirement. It's a detriment. Instead, patience, desire, and persistence are the requisites.

My experience with those recovering from eating disorders reveals a journey of self-discovery, courage, and transformation—one well worth taking, even if it doesn't feel as such.

Stephanie Klein, RD, LDN, RYT

We live in a culture that glorifies restriction and restrictive eating patterns. For this reason, it can feel "normal" to have food rules and restrictive behaviors. In a sense, our current culture has its own eating disorder, making it difficult for people to seek support.

The younger population faces the challenge of being exposed to disordered eating from social media, where it is glorified. Therefore, they do not feel they need help.

As a dietitian working with the eating disorder population, I see many clients struggle with not feeling "sick enough" for treatment. It often takes many years of battling the disorder before seeking professional assistance.

The reality is it is never too early to seek support even if someone has grappled with an eating disorder or disordered eating for a short period. Supports, which might include friends, family, a therapist, dietitian, and psychiatrist, care about one's recovery, not about the journey's ups and downs.

Think about the following statements and consider if or how they apply to you:

I always think about my weight.

I worry about the food I put into my body out of fear of gaining weight.

I have a poor body image.

I have rules for eating certain foods.

I have an unhealthy relationship with food.

The truth is it is NOT natural to continually think about food, food choices, weight, and your body. If you do, you deserve freedom and support.

Although it may feel comfortable to avoid certain foods, I would encourage you to reassess your relationship with it unless there is a medical reason, such as an allergy.

Eating disorders are incredibly complex, but they do not require a diagnosis to seek professional guidance and treatment. For this reason, no matter what others are struggling with, YOU deserve to get help for your eating disorder or disordered eating. You are worthy of freedom from food rules, having a healthy relationship with food and your body, and experiencing pleasure with eating.

My clients are beyond resilient, strong, and determined. I feel blessed to be a part of their journey and am honored to work with each of them.

If I could give one piece of advice to those suffering from an eating disorder or disordered eating, it would be to reach out for help despite how uncomfortable or challenging it feels.

Table of Contents

Introduction ... 13

## Section I	Treatment

The Vase ... 19
Alexandra And ED ... 24
Speak Up ... 27
Swimming With My Fears ... 33
What Happens Next? ... 36
Graduation From Treatment - The Next Step In Recovery ... 38

## Section II	Comfortable Being Uncomfortable

Imprisoned By Fear ... 40
Which Voice Will You Listen To? ... 43
Why Bother? ... 45
F**k It ... 48
I Think I Can ... 50
ED Is Crying ... 52
Let's Make A Deal ... 54

## Section III	Living In The Now

NOW ... 56
In The Moment ... 60
Stress = I'm Not Hungry ... 63
Where's Me Time? ... 66
Time To Walk ... 69

## Section IV	Mental Circles

Mental Merry-Go-Round ... 72
Watch Out! She's Going To Blow! ... 75
Too Much ... 77
Cycles Of Trouble ... 79
Magnifying Glass ... 81
Running On Empty ... 83

It's Always The Same	85
Drowning	87
The Bench	90

Section V   Wearing A Mask

Perceptions Are Deceiving	92
Feeling Lonely	95
Gray Skies	97
Ouch!	100
Digging For Feelings	103
In A Fix	106
BINGO	109
Behind The Mask	112
The Show Must Go On	115

Section VI   F**k ED

Audrey And ED	117
The Evil Scale	121
What The Hell Happened?	125
Unlock The Door	129
Just Go To Sleep	133
Now Playing	135
Change... It's Time For One	137
Hurdles	139
Do You See What I See?	142
May I Take Your Order?	145
How Dare You!	148
The Endless Debate	150

Section VII   False Sense Of Control

To Eat Or Not To Eat	152
Yeah! I Am Imperfect	155
High Jump Of Expectations	157
Yard Sale	159
Power Struggle	161
Where In The World Is Matt Lauer?	163
Self-Preservation	166

Blah! Blah!	169
Sleeping Beauty	172

Section VIII Build A Toolbox

Helpful Tools In My Recovery	177
10 Minutes… 10 Minutes	180
Do The Next Right Thing	183
Jet Airways	185
Life Is Like The Weather	187
FUN	189
To-Do List	192
You Found Me	194
Drama In Your Life	196
Cookie Jar	198
Boxing	200
Filling Your Tank	203
Christian Grey	205
A Posse Of One	207
Above The Line	210
I Have No Patience	213
Recovery Bank	216
Balance Of Hope	220

Section IX Wrapping It Up… Or Am I?

What's Inside The Windows?	223
Miss You, Dad	228

Section X Bonus Entries

I'm Stuck!	232
Loss Comes In Many Forms	237
I'm Fine	241
The Box	245
Basic Math	250
Seesaw Of Needs	253
No Escape: Smothered	261
What About Me?	264
Tea For One	268

Section XI   Wrapping It Up... This Time I Mean It

Romance Titles Faith Starr	276
About Faith Elicia	277
Please Review My Book	278
Musical Inspiration	279
Help And Support Are Available	281
Acknowledgments	283
Workbook Copyrights	285

Introduction

My journey along the path of recovery from my eating disorder is similar to a dance. And by that, I am not referring to a tango you would see on *Dancing With The Stars*. I am talking about stepping on your partner's feet or forgetting choreography in front of an audience—a blooper you would view on *America's Funniest Home Videos*. It is a dance with poor direction, a slow learning curve, falls, bruises, and a perfect pirouette every now and then.

Recovery from an eating disorder is in no way, shape, or form graceful. It is bumpy and rigorous. It is the most challenging feat I have had to endure so far. That includes child-rearing. I get breaks from my kids, not my eating disorder. It is like an abusive friend who finds joy when I suffer, a bully in every sense of the word.

My eating disorder has been a hundred times more draining, let alone more emotionally exhausting, than raising my three kids. I reap many benefits from being a mother. The eating disorder has given me none. Zip. Even if it tells me otherwise.

So why bother to recover if it takes so much effort? And to put it mildly, the process stinks.

Because there is no alternative if I want to live, not just exist, either, I'm talking live a fulfilling life.

So far, my recovery has been a roller coaster of ups, downs, twists, turns, and backward movement. The blessing is that the ride continues. It never stops moving, which means I always get another chance to buckle up for another attempt.

Gaining awareness about my detrimental behaviors, triggers, and thoughts that invariably lead to self-destruction enhances my understanding of distinguishing when my eating disorder is taking the reins and steering versus my healthy, pro-recovery voice.

Am I where I want to be in my recovery?

My inner voice yells, "Hell, no!"

My compassionate voice says, "You are where you are," with no judgment.

Each day brings new lessons to learn and grow from. When I look back, I can say I am farther along the road to health than when I first started this journey, including the tumbles and falls. The difference today is I get up quicker.

This book has remained shelved because whenever I got the urge to move forward with it, I negated the idea with the rationale that publishing it would be hypocritical. I mean, how could I publish a book about eating disorder recovery when I am not fully recovered?

I have since changed my views because I believe recovery is a lifelong process. Others believe in full recovery—*recovered*. I won't comment on it one way or the other. I can only speak for myself, and in my case, recovery comes one day at a time.

Am I frustrated because I should be "fixed" by now? Yes. But then I reframe the critical self-talk cycles that repeat in my head. Beating myself up doesn't work. It only makes things worse.

This path has taken me down many roads. I have gone to support groups and read books on eating disorder recovery. I journal, engage in cognitive-behavioral therapy, see a dietitian, and follow a spiritual path. As a result, I have discovered I have a lot to live and be grateful for. I get one shot at life, and I want to make it a worthwhile and productive one.

Making a difference is vital. I am hopeful this workbook will make a positive impact on someone's life. If it does, I have succeeded. If it doesn't, no harm done. I have faced my shame and put myself out there, thus, nourishing myself in the process—pun intended.

This leads to my next point: I am thankful for my eating disorder.

Did I really just say that?

It's crazy, right?

Not in this instance. If I hadn't suffered so immensely, I would have never had the opportunity to soul-search and figure out who I am, what I need, what I want, and most importantly, that I have a voice and deserve to use it.

My journey of recovery began when I entered a partial hospitalization program. After having my third child, I had grave difficulty handling the stress of a newborn, bundled with all my other work and household duties. My eating disorder had been around for years but never to the point of obsession where it interfered with my daily life and became dangerous. How quickly that changed.

Sensing my despair, my eating disorder, who from here on out I will refer to as ED, leached on to me and tried to drown me. It became so severe my psychiatrist discharged me because of the liability involved. He recommended I see an eating disorder specialist because he could no longer be of service to me.

Devastation.

It is the only word to describe how I felt. Being a person who fears rejection, that experience did a number on me. How could the man throw me to the curb so easily? A man I trusted with my innermost thoughts. A man whose office was an hour away from my home. An office I couldn't drive to because of crippling anxiety. My husband had to schedule work breaks to get me to my appointments. And still, the doctor released me as a patient.

It didn't take long to realize my psychiatrist did me a favor. I am eternally grateful for his wisdom.

I entered treatment within two weeks of being discharged because I could no longer breathe—figurately. ED was destroying me minute by minute, hour by hour, day by day. I'd had enough. It was time to seize back control of my life.

During the partial hospitalization program (PHP), I used art as an outlet for my feelings. My drawings took on a whole new meaning when I journaled about them.

Each section moving forward will display the actual artwork I created during and following treatment, along with some newer drawings.

I warn you, a Picasso, I'm not. That doesn't mean I don't cherish my perfectly imperfect art because it benefited me tremendously, rescued me, in a sense. My wish is to inspire others to take the scary nosedive into the unknown world of recovery.

Following each picture is a journal entry that corresponds to the drawing. When necessary, I give brief explanations for clarification purposes. These personal reflection sections are titled: My Turn.

I advise readers to proceed with caution as some entries discuss ED behaviors. I will give a heads-up under the name of the journal entry. I, in no way, mean to trigger. My journey thus far has come from years of internal pain, shame, and suffering. My past has led me to my now.

Where necessary, I have changed names for the protection and confidentiality of my family.

It has been my experience that recovery doesn't happen in isolation. I am not a physician or therapist. All information presented is based on my journey. The suggestions made are those that have worked for me. Take what works for you and leave the rest behind.

This workbook is not a replacement for medical treatment. I **strongly** encourage anyone suffering from an eating disorder to seek medical care from a psychiatrist, therapist, and nutritionist, all of whom specialize in eating disorders. I can't stress this concept enough. Eating disorders are deadly.

Before entering treatment, I saw a therapist two to three times a week to get back on track. It didn't nor couldn't work because the woman knew nothing about eating disorders. In hindsight, she enabled my sickness to progress, unlike the psychiatrist who took a stand.

Eating disorders are masters at manipulating others—us included—to see what they want us to see.

After my entries is a section titled: Your Turn. It is here where I ask you to consider the topic presented and how it relates to you. It might. It might not. All I ask is for you to be open-minded.

This workbook can be ongoing, the entries revisited, as we are in perpetual movement and will think differently about the same concepts depending on our internal state of affairs.

The most important thing to remember is that no two eating disorders look the same, so **don't** compare. My story is mine. Yours is yours. We all hit different bottoms and jump on the bandwagon of recovery at different stages in our eating disorders.

When you see an asterisk break in entries, you will see the words: Add-on during editing. These are newer perspectives on my original entries. This workbook covers a span of seven years. Most of the entries took place when I was fresh in recovery (2013-2014). There are intermittent others. The last section includes newer entries.

If you are prepared to take the leap of faith into the beautiful, painful, and unpredictable journey of recovery, which I hope you are, let's get started.

First and foremost, I'd like to introduce myself and share some personal information before getting to the nitty-gritty. The following is a brief list of things I openly share with others:

I am a mother of three.

I am a dog lover and own four dogs. I had two during most of my initial drawings: Sammy (Silky Terrier) and Toby (Westie). You will notice Rudy (Rescue Mix) and Jack (Black Schnauzer Rescue) in the newer drawings.

I've been married for 26 years and counting.

I hold a BS in Communication.

I hold a MS in Education.

I am a contemporary romance writer with more than eight titles to my name.

I manage my husband's medical practice.

I am a certified hypnotist, which I find cool.

I am certified in Reiki I and II, which I perform on myself regularly.

I completed the 8-week Mindfulness-Based Stress Reduction Program within a year of this publication, and it's been a life-changer.

I completed the 8-week Mindful Self-Compassion Program while editing this workbook.

My family is my everything.

Spirituality has become my way of life.

I hate to toot my own horn, but I sound surprisingly good on paper, don't you think?

Not to diminish or belittle my accomplishments, which I've worked extremely hard to achieve, but here is a list of things I don't openly share with others:

I am an adult child of an alcoholic.

I am codependent and attend Codependency Anonymous meetings.

I suffer from Generalized Anxiety and Panic Disorder.

I suffer from an eating disorder – Anorexia Nervosa, to be specific.

I thrive in isolation, which is conducive to being an author. What's not conducive is that this lifestyle has become a protective means to keep me emotionally safe. Simply put, my social circle is the size of a quarter.

This workbook is about being honest. I don't sugarcoat or exaggerate recovery. It is in my truth where self-discovery has become possible, and I have been able to catch glimpses of recovery.

Ready to get down to business?

If so, please join me, and let's get to it.

Section I
Treatment

The Vase

My Turn

What is Art Therapy, and how will it aid in my recovery from my eating disorder?

After spending Tuesday afternoons and Wednesday mornings during treatment in a group specifically dedicated to art, I quickly got the answers.

At first, I thought Art Therapy was a waste. Why devote an entire group to it? I mean, seriously, what could I possibly learn about myself by exploring my emotions through art? Sure, I knew it was a useful therapeutic tool to use with kids, but adults? Nah. I didn't buy it.

Art is a form of expression, the same as singing and writing—two of my passions. The latter creative outlets have effectively released pent-up emotions and repressed pain, internal suffering, and sadness. When it came to art, I had a disconnect in using it for healing properties.

How wrong my first impression turned out to be.

Sherry, the art therapist at the treatment center, would present a theme for the patients to ponder and illustrate. Instead of following directions, I chose to draw about something different. Interestingly, rather than get reprimanded for being disobedient, my originality was encouraged and praised. Sherry commended me for following my instincts as her suggestions were mere prompts to inspire us. That kicked my enthusiasm up a level or two.

Paint, crayons, markers, and the like, were placed sporadically around the table.

After a failed attempt at painting and a trial of colored chalk, which resulted in a masterpiece of smeared colors, I changed gears. My tools of choice became colored pencils and permanent markers.

I soon realized this Art Therapy thing had something to it. Even better, I enjoyed it and looked forward to it. So much so, I woke up extra early to meditate about a topic I read in the reflections book, *Words of Courage and Confidence*, by Sue Patton Thoele, then drew a picture related to it.

Fortunately, I work for my husband, so my schedule is flexible. Being I have no help at home with the kids and have a job that requires dedicated time and attention, I found a program that suited my needs.

It amazed me how much I could get done in a twenty-four-hour period when I had a set schedule in place. Imagine that? Time management has never been my forte.

My morning routine became a reference point for many of my drawings and journal entries as the days progressed into weeks, months, and years.

The idea of drawing a vase came from a meditation about filling our life's vase before filling those of others.

This concept was worth investigating because I easily give until my tank is empty without filling it in return. The result is physical, mental, and emotional exhaustion. My eating disorder thrives in that type of internal environment.

The strategies I've learned in recovery have taught me how to refill my tank. I'm referring to self-care, which is paramount when recovering from an eating disorder.

My vase represents my being.

The inside includes things that enlighten me from within, such as music, singing, nature, the sun, the beach, and writing.

The outside includes things in my immediate surroundings that make me happy, like my family, my dogs—even though they drive me crazy—my home office where I not only work but write my romance novels, and my home in general.

All of these things, both inside and out, are what fill me daily.

Unfortunately, it can also be the opposite. The external things can also create an excessive amount of tension and anxiety instead.

The more centered I am, the better equipped I am at handling external stressors and situations. Unfortunately, many outside factors heighten my anxiety. Inner peace doesn't come easily. Like anything else, it takes work and practice, and some days I'm in a better place than others.

The easiest method for me to become grounded is to meditate. The more frequently I engage in it, the more inner peace I find. That's not to say symptoms of anxiety and all of my worries vanish. It merely means I'm better able to handle life on life's terms.

The sun represents my inner light, which makes my flowers and inner-self bloom.

Your Turn

If you were to draw a vase to represent your life, what would it look like?

It doesn't have to be a vase. It can be a cup or mug—anything you want as long as it's something you can fill. Remember, keep an open mind. This is your activity, nobody else's.

What would fill your vase, or whatever else you choose?

What would be on the outside of it?

Reflect on these ideas. Draw, write, sing, talk, meditate, or anything else that might motivate you to explore them.

When it comes to recovery, we have to find what works for us individually. There is no right or wrong way to approach it unless it's doing it on our own. That's a no-no.

Consider the things that make you unique and special from within. You might only come up with one thing, and on another trial come up with an entire list. And if you end up empty-handed, that's okay, too. Give it time, and more importantly, be patient with yourself. Our eating disorders didn't happen overnight, and neither does recovery.

Discovery is part of the process. Beating yourself up is not allowed when working on any of the suggested activities in this workbook. Again, if one doesn't sit right with you, scrap it and try a different one. Hell, make up one of your own. Permit yourself to let your creativity shine and run wild.

The examples you choose should include things about yourself that make the cheerleader inside of you shout, "Hurray for me!"

Challenge yourself to find at least one thing that fills you on the inside. If you come up with many, I bow down to you. Either way, giving it a go—even if solely reading through the entries for a taste of the content—is a reward in itself. Pat yourself on the back for taking a risk and engaging in self-care. Welcome to the road of recovery.

Next, explore the people, places, and things that bring you joy from the outside.

These need to be productive. Sorry ED, you are excluded from this party. It doesn't belong anywhere near this vase or item of your choosing. It might seem as if your eating disorder is filling or consuming you, but that isn't the reality of the situation.

The outside stuff was a lot easier for me to brainstorm.

Armed with this detailed list in the art-form of your choosing, what will you choose to fill yourself with today?

Which one thing, whether from within or without, can help you make it a day that stands out from the rest and allows your flowers to bloom just a little bit more?

I'm not talking leaps and bounds. Some days we need to water our flowers more than others. Only you know how much water is necessary daily.

Why not give it a try? You already know how it feels to fill yourself with your eating disorder. How is that working for you? I'm going to go out on a limb and say not well based on my enmeshed relationship with mine. Why not try something new and different?

Please keep in mind that you will never hear me say the process of recovery is easy.

Worth it? Yes.

A must? Absolutely.

Alexandra And ED

My Turn

Many balloons in my life keep me afloat. Like my vase, they are the things from both within and outside of me that bring me happiness.

Alexandra is a name I came up with years ago to represent my inner light. She gives me strength, hope, and courage.

Unfortunately, she doesn't visit often. My incessant worries keep her tucked away, but she will make an unexpected appearance, and I get assurance all will be well. She's what keeps me moving forward when my feet get stuck in cement, and I feel as if I can't take another step.

The bricks weigh me down. They represent fear, anxiety (whom I named Audrey), control, and ED. I could sum up all of the bricks under one heading: fear.

My fears increase the bricks' weight, and it becomes almost impossible to move an inch in the right direction. The impetus to try and control everything around me, whether it be another person, life circumstance, or other external factor, is an impossible feat. The result is overwhelming powerlessness and utter exhaustion.

In all actuality, the only things within my power are my reactions to people and events and how I *choose* to look at situations as they present themselves.

This realization is both freeing and imprisoning.

I can relax with the awareness that others will do as they wish, and things will take place that I have no say in. However, my inner voice responds with, "Look what's going on around me. I need to fix it."

The feelings that build due to this lack of control can become so overpowering that I control the one thing I can, engaging in self-destructive ED behaviors.

The bricks holding me down are by no means grounding. They do the opposite. They bury me and keep me stuck.

Your Turn

What are your bricks? What things in your life are holding you back from finding inner peace?

It might not look like I have many bricks in my drawing but trust me when I say each one weighs a ton squared.

What are your balloons? What things in your life lift you?

You might only have one balloon. If that's the case, make it sparkle to give it extra lifting power.

What can you do to release a brick and allow your balloon(s) to pull you up and out of your head?

I have found walking through my fears, big and small, lightens the weight of my bricks. Once I accomplish a task with success, it gets easier to repeat. The most significant benefit is the pride I get from my accomplishment. Alexandra will usually smile and give me a thumb's up for a job well done.

I will admit I often don't succeed in my first or second attempt. All I ask of myself is progress. My strive for perfection is what causes ED to rear its ugly head, to begin with. I will gladly take progress over the perfection that doesn't exist any day.

Explore these ideas in a manner that works best for you, or try something different. Maybe you will discover a secret Rembrandt has been hiding inside of you, or even better, a Katy Perry, who can turn your bricks into balloons with a song. Can I hear you "Roar"?

You'll never know the endless possibilities within your reach if you don't try and grab some.

Speak Up

My Turn

ED behaviors discussed. Read with caution.

My husband and oldest son argued. I intervened and used my voice. I couldn't take being silent any longer, sitting by and listening to the disrespect taking place toward my son on behalf of his father without a peep from me.

It was a HUGE step. I usually remain quiet during conflicts.

My son and husband have no trouble voicing their opinions to each other and then letting it go as if nothing happened.

Me? I'm not as effective at letting go.

My husband had his hearing checked because he says he can never hear me. It turned out to be perfectly fine. It's the tone of my voice, not his hearing, that's the problem. I grew up with the message that I didn't deserve to be heard. It's a classic symptom of being an adult child of an alcoholic.

The following is an assignment that a therapist in my treatment group gave to me. It's about finding out who I am since I somehow lost track of myself along the way.

I turned the assignment into a poem, something I often do as a writer. Following the poem are two additional prompts and the responses I gave.

Who Am I?

A little girl with pig-tales, braids that mommy made,

A father whom I feared, my bedroom was where I stayed.

Singing in my room became my way to cope,

It gave me strength and courage. It always gave me hope.

Yelling or dictating orders was how our house was run,

Not allowed to speak loudly or laugh. How dare we have such fun?

Searching for answers; thinking all dads had to be bad,

Men were always angry; they just made you feel sad.

Mom was the savior. She protected me from it all,

Not allowing me to experience the real world, sheltering me from a fall.

But how would I survive without her? Survive this world without her by my side?

How would I succeed on my own without inner strength or pride?

Capable I always was, the good child who did no wrong,

The perfect little girl who always cheered Mom up with a song.

My sisters? They were the ones with the problems. I didn't want those for me,

In a search to find myself and grow up came a life filled with anxiety.

My life story:

(There have been slight modifications for anonymity purposes)

A family with five daughters and two parents who worked nonstop.

Alcoholism/addiction in a few of its members.

My oldest sister almost died in a tragic car accident when I was in ninth grade. I still have a paralyzing fear of hospitals and doctors after seeing what my sister went through in the ICU and her year-long recovery afterward.

I thought my family was typical. After all, everybody has secrets. But in my family, *everything* was a secret. We weren't allowed to discuss family issues with outsiders. The problems we had within our house's walls were ours and ours alone, not intended for others to hear. They were shameful.

My dad was mean. All fathers were. Weren't they?

In my mind, they were.

Work was my mother's escape.

She was and shall remain my role model, a strong-willed survivor.

How did she do it? How could she be so resilient with all the craziness going on around her?

She always gave of herself to her children, especially me. But deep down, work came first. It always did. At least, that was how I perceived it.

I am the baby of the group. I stayed close to home even when I should have ventured off. I went to a local university but, unfortunately, had an anxiety-ridden breakdown during my final semester of undergrad. I withdrew without graduating. That came later.

I became agoraphobic. That kept me safe from having to go out into the world and do things on my own.

My parents owned a business, and I had always worked for them. There was security in being the bosses' child. I hated working for them because of my dad's mood swings, but it enabled me to function in a so-called "safe" place.

As a youth, I went to sleepaway camp one summer and experienced terrible separation anxiety.

As an older teen, I traveled to New York to promote my demo tapes with a possible manager. I suffered such tremendous anxiety I had to return home, giving up a possible chance of a lifetime.

I found another calling while getting my master's degree. I worked at the campus preschool and loved being with the kids. They made me happy. They were full of life and found pleasure in the simplest of things. They made me stop and appreciate the little things as well.

My husband was my fiancé during that period, and he had faith in me. He still does. He motivated me to finish undergrad and continue with grad school, both of which I did.

He has walked this journey alongside me, either in front of me—reaching out a hand to pull me forward—or behind me—encouraging me to take a blind step in the right direction.

I remember him holding my hand while we waited for our turn in the deli line at the market, which could feel like an eternity. For me, it was such an anxiety-provoking event.

When one struggles with severe panic and anxiety, everything can seem like an eternity until returning to a so-called safe place.

In those types of scenarios, which presented themselves frequently, he would simply remind me to breathe deeply, going so far as to do so with me, to bring me back into the moment.

There are days he believes in me more than I believe in myself. He is the only real friend I have ever had who loves me unconditionally. He will encourage me to branch out but won't enable or protect me as my mom did.

I will admit there are moments I walk in his shadow, behind all his confidence.

He is strong. I admire his strength. His love provides me with a sense of importance and belonging.

He tells me I can do things I don't feel capable of.

I need to become the him in my life. I need to believe in myself the way he believes in me.

Other negative beliefs and messages rattling in my mind:

Writing has and always will be a way for me to express myself.

Writing poems enables me to release repressed emotions.

Singing enables me to let go of them.

Writing romance fiction enables me to escape to unknown places where I set the stage and make magic happen.

Unfortunately, exercise enables me to purge my feelings.

As I wrote my story, I didn't want to rehash all the incidents from my past. The central theme that stood out was a lack of confidence in myself. It is evident in all I do.

All of my anxiety and fears come from self-doubt. My successes come at a price. They come with the pressure I put on myself beforehand to complete them, only to over-excel and make sure they're done to perfection. I must be the perfect mother, wife, daughter, etc.

From where does this perfectionism come?

From me, that's where. If I do things perfectly, maybe it will make me more lovable in all the roles I play. If I please those around me, then all will be peaceful. God forbid someone gets upset with me.

Aren't these valid assumptions—the "if this" and "if that"?

It's always "if."

Your Turn

Don't be afraid to use your voice—easy for me to say, not do. It's the best weapon we have to face the world as we perceive it and free ourselves from our silent hell.

Make your needs known. We were given voices for a reason, and they deserve to be heard, even when we speak in decibels only animals can hear.

How can you use your voice to assert your needs and wants?

First and foremost, what are your needs and wants?

It might take some soul-searching to come up with them. Later in the workbook is an activity that describes individual needs in greater detail.

If you want to challenge yourself and do the assignment I completed, feel free to do so. The first part is to define who you are—your make-up, your family dynamic, and who you have become.

If you do this task, please do so under the guidance of a professional. Many emotions arose when I completed these assignments, but I could process them in a group since I was in treatment.

The intent of this activity isn't to provoke eating disorder behaviors. Its purpose is to identify feelings and create awareness.

The second part of the assignment is to determine other negative beliefs and messages rattling in your mind.

These are heavy and loaded prompts. Proceed with caution. The major take-home from this entry is to use your voice. It matters. It counts. It has something worthwhile to contribute.

If you think this is nonsense, I will repeat it. Use your voice. It matters. It counts. It has something worthwhile to contribute.

Repeat the paragraph above as often as necessary until it sinks in.

Swimming With My Fears

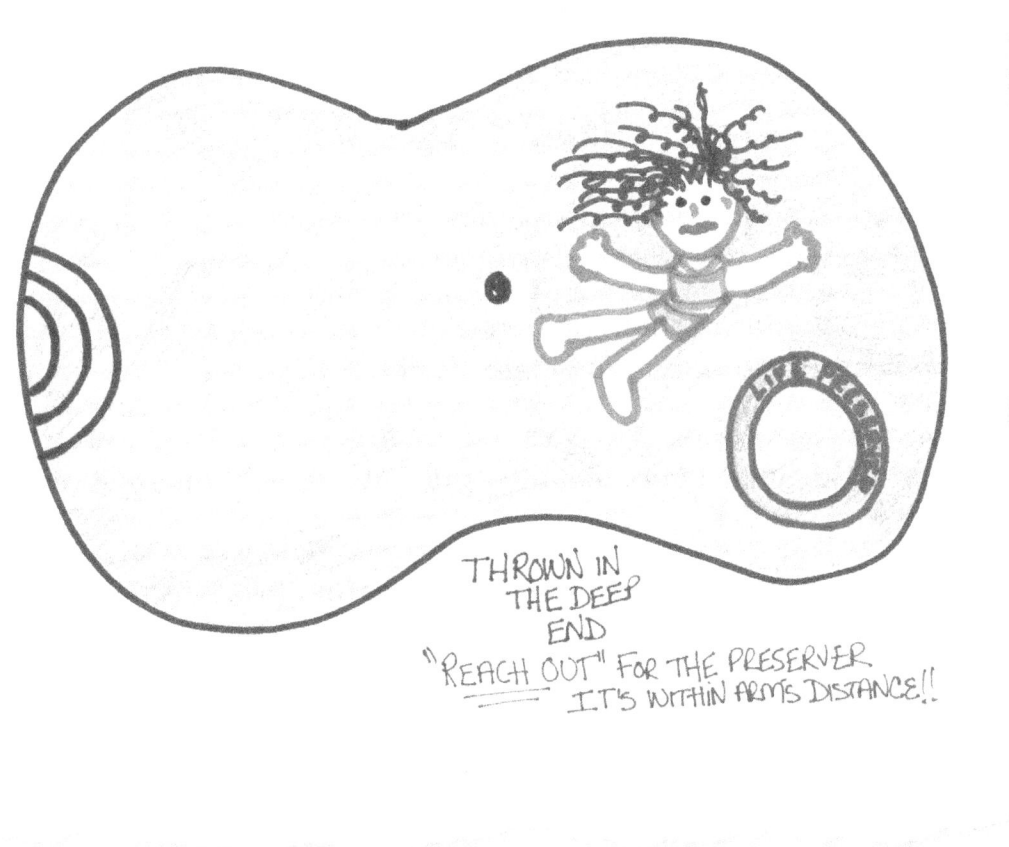

THROWN IN THE DEEP END
"REACH OUT" FOR THE PRESERVER
— IT'S WITHIN ARMS DISTANCE!!

My Turn

I feel as if I've been thrown into a pool and can't swim, and the life preserver is just beyond my reach.

My treatment center informed me that my full-time status is pending because of my insurance benefits. I was taken aback by this news.

This fear of change caused my ED voice to revisit. It seems like my mind has the uncanny ability to reset itself to old ways of thinking whenever the unexpected transpires.

It has been days since I've had compulsions to act out with ED, which worsens the circumstances. I know things will work out, but my initial reaction is to fear the unknown instead of viewing the "problem" as an opportunity for growth.

I added quotes to the word *problem* during editing because a situation is what I make of it and how I view it.

Your Turn

What can you do if you get thrown into a pool of the unknown—pretend you can't swim to make the activity worthwhile?

It might be a change of thought, behavior, or anything else that can inspire you to look at the situation in a different light.

Life always throws curveballs. We need to be skilled athletes to catch them. Recovery makes us Olympian Gold Medalists. Never underestimate your ability.

Utilizing the lists of strategies and tools we've made in other entries can be reviewed and practiced when confronted with perceived scary unknowns.

We can pause before going into fight or flight mode.

We can meditate about upcoming changes to gain a better perspective of them.

We can view them as lessons to learn from as we challenge ourselves to walk through our fears.

We can be honest about our insecurities and self-doubt with a trusted friend, partner, or therapist.

We don't have to go at it alone.

Remaining stuck in our heads is probably the worst possible tactic to use when faced with change. The ED voice loves to creep in during vulnerable and weak moments of internal doubt, possibly without our awareness.

ED is conniving and manipulative, which is why external support is crucial. Isolating and withdrawing—two of my favorites—should not be options when confronted with unpleasant stressors.

Write about your feelings.

Draw about them.

Talk about and share them with a trusted person in your life.

Never forget we are only alone when we choose to be. We are only as lonely as we allow ourselves to feel.

What Happens Next?

My Turn

I've decided to leave the safety and security of treatment. I've gained all I can and will continue my recovery path in the real world using my treatment team's assistance.

Fear comes along with this decision. Mostly, I'm afraid to revert to old ways of thinking and behaving. It would be a no-brainer to forget all I have learned since the tools are new, and many of them unpracticed. They are not habitual like my ED behaviors are.

I will leave with a new understanding of myself, my behaviors, the family dynamic in my home, and how all of these things affect me.

Your Turn

Where are you at this stage in your recovery?

Where do you see progress?

You aren't allowed to say there isn't any. Reaching this point in this workbook is progress, even if you haven't worked through all of the activities.

What behaviors, if any, have you had success in changing?

Which ones still need work?

What are you learning about yourself along this journey?

Remember to praise even the tiniest changes because they can turn out to be the biggest and most rewarding ones.

Graduation From Treatment – The Next Step In Recovery

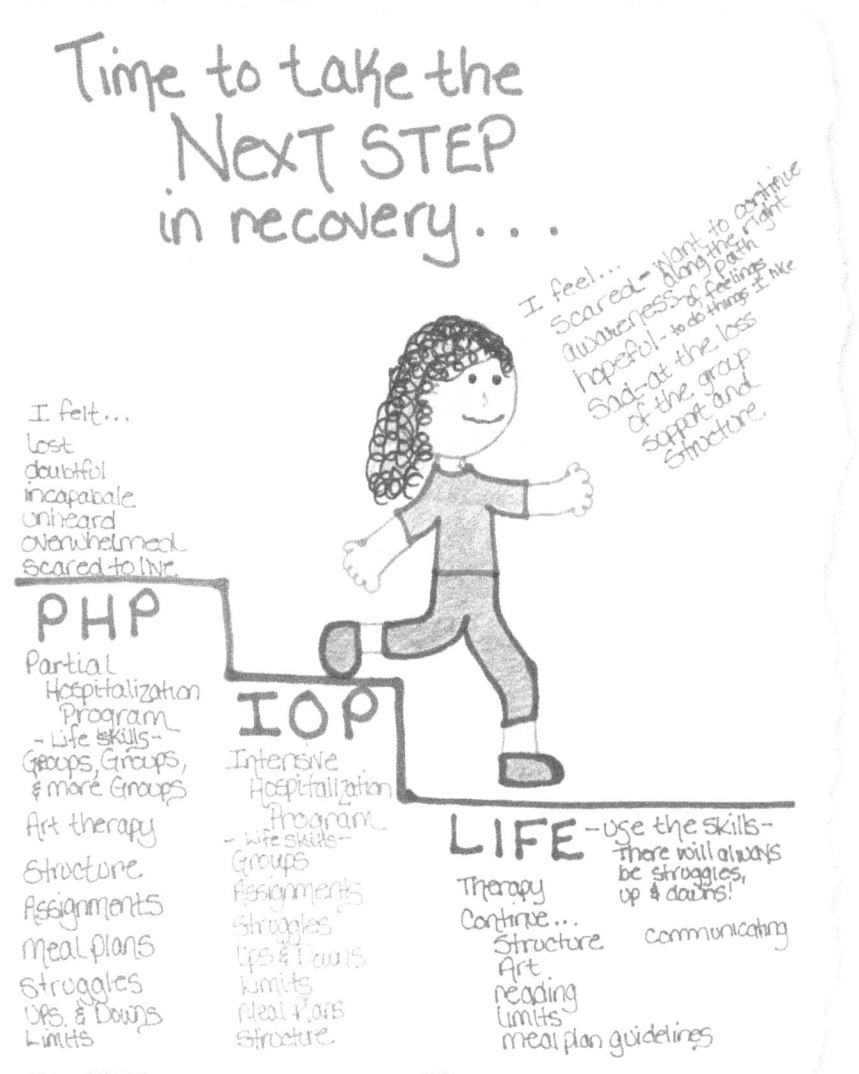

My Turn

I put all of the writing assignments I completed over the past few months into my treatment binder. It was bittersweet.

Treatment gave me a safe forum to share my feelings, talk to others going through similar experiences, provided structure, and gave me laughs between the tears. It was gratifying to receive acceptance for who I am. It also reconnected me with others.

After getting pregnant with my third child and being on bed rest for months, I became isolated and cutoff from society. Treatment gave me tools to re-enter it while allowing me to explore the reasons behind why I seclude myself: fear of rejection and abandonment.

It's humbling to see positive changes. It hasn't been a walk in the park. Recovering on my own was a failure, the same as working with the ignorant therapist. Fortunately, treatment provided some degree of success.

I have appointments scheduled with a new therapist and dietitian who specialize in eating disorders and my psychiatrist.

Recovery hasn't been monumental steps of victories. Instead, it's been turtle steps forward and backward. The falls sometimes push me ahead, or the opposite occurs. I keep dusting off my pants and trying again.

Your Turn

What steps have you taken to conquer your eating disorder?

Do you believe you can recover alone?

If yes, how has that worked in your favor, if at all?

Who are your supports in recovery?

I can't stress enough the importance of surrounding yourself with accepting people who can understand and relate to what you are going through.

The Help And Support Are Available section at the end of the workbook provides information on where and how to find professional support.

Section II
Comfortable Being Uncomfortable

Imprisoned By Fear

My Turn

It feels like I'm serving a life sentence for worry, control, and fear. Self-doubt imprisons me. The "what ifs" and "shoulds" keep me stuck in a pit of doom and gloom, and it becomes almost impossible to get hold of the key, which will release me from a self-destructive cycle. It's always one step out of my reach.

I'm learning in recovery that taking one step forward, and then another, will lead me toward my goal of finding self-love, peace, and balance. The pot of gold will be the gift I receive at the end of the rainbow for freeing myself from ED's life sentence.

Even when I take a step backward or fall, the footprints of hard work that I've already walked have become solidified, so I'm never back where I started. I simply—wrong choice of words because recovery isn't simple—resume my position where I stumbled off my path and continue toward the pot of gold, which, on many occasions, seems lightyears away.

At times it appears as if there has been no progress, but once awareness sets in, it alerts me when I'm running back to the presumed safety of old self-deceiving thoughts and beliefs. In other words, the jail sentence in my head.

Your Turn

What's imprisoning you in your life—what's keeping you locked up with self-defeating thoughts?

For me, it usually has something to do with fear and powerlessness, fear of the unknown, or fear of a loss of control. I prefer the familiar comfort of discomfort rather than taking a risk and trying something new and different because it's all I know. Insight tells me this type of thinking will keep me locked up with Audrey and ED.

In every second of every minute, the key to unlocking the jail cell I reside in hangs within arm's reach. All that's necessary is my willingness to grab it, open the gate, and step into the sunlight.

This is easier said than done, but the only way to recover from ED is to take that initial step forward.

Sometimes I make bold choices for someone else, like my husband or nutritionist, when I don't have the motivation to make them for myself.

Today I know it's okay to make changes I don't like or agree with on behalf of someone else with the knowledge that at some point, I'll choose to do the right thing for myself instead.

Whatever motivates us to take a step forward is all that matters. Eventually, we will take these steps because they make us feel better and, in reality, more **in** control of our lives.

What fancy footwork can you bring to your step that will get you closer to the pot of gold that awaits you?

The pot of gold may seem close on some days and others eons away.

Keep in mind that we all get a taste or glimpse of freedom from ED with each step forward, time, and patience.

If you can't recover for yourself today, why not do it for someone or something else—like your pet who loves you unconditionally or that picture of your little self in the second-grade yearbook when your mother styled your hair like Princess Leia's. Oh, wait, I'm referring to myself. I still have the photo as proof, too. Ah, memories.

Just take that step.

Which Voice Will You Listen To?

My Turn

There are times I feel I'm on the right track only to realize I'm not. Will I ever find solace in feeling content?

When stressors arise, the first voice I hear is ED's, telling me it knows what's best for me, or it can be sneaky. It will persuade me to act out before I even realize what has happened.

My recovery voice will ask me how I can make things right. It knows what's best for me in the long run, not the "quick fix" ED insists it provides.

Visualizing a little angel on one shoulder and a little devil on the other has been effective. Both of them tell me what to do, but which one will I listen to?

The choice is mine even though I recurrently succumb to ED's peer pressure.

Your Turn

Which voice will you listen to, the little angel or the little devil?

Can you decipher between the two?

Which voices are trying to hurt you?

Those are the little devils.

Try to distinguish between them as they race around in your mind. With recognition between ED's voice and your recovery voice comes the power to fight back.

I still listen to ED periodically. I accept I am human and make mistakes. Belittling myself or engaging in more ED behaviors doesn't make the situation better. On the contrary, it makes it worse. Doing the next right thing yields more promising rewards.

Why Bother?

My Turn

ED behaviors discussed. Read with caution.

I haven't had the itch to draw in a while. I reread the *Fifty Shades Trilogy*, and it was just as enticing as my first read-through. I haven't seen my nutritionist in a month or my therapist in three weeks.

Life has a knack for getting in the way of things.

The more I disconnect from my supports, the more I fall prey to ED. How easy it is to resort to old behaviors. They are familiar. They are what I know.

My rationale is that as long as I maintain a healthy weight, it doesn't matter if I restrict. My husband tends to disagree. He tells me it's not about the number on the scale. Rather, it's about my relationship with food. What is he, my f**king nutritionist now? But he's right, and I know it.

I spoke with him and our older son about life. I told my son he's lucky to be at a stage where the sky is the limit. He can do whatever he wants with his future.

The discussion turned philosophical in that my son discussed how insignificant we are in the grand scheme of things, and when we pass, nothing will keep our memory alive unless we do something "big."

I explained to him that life is what we make it.

To me, the "big" is the things we do that fill us. It's the ability to look back and be satisfied with where we've been. Not all of us will get recognition like Elvis, but then again, was he genuinely happy? Isn't it better to live than simply be remembered?

I was ordering back-to-school books on Amazon during our discussion, and I came across something interesting. It was one of those meant-to-be moments that summed up our conversation about life. I'm adding it here because it's so relevant. The synopsis of the epic series, *The Universe Doesn't Give a Flying F**k About You* by Johnny B. Truant, as copied from Amazon, is below.

****

"If you walk around every day on eggshells, nervous about making a mistake or looking stupid, then you should read this.

If you have a "next big thing" in mind you want to do because you know it will be awesome (starting the business, making the big move, launching the nonprofit, writing the book) but are afraid of doing what it would take to make that thing happen, then you should read this.

The universe is big. You are small. In fact, you're so small and so insignificant in the big picture that you don't even register to the eye of the cosmos. The universe was here before you were born and will be here long after you're gone, and your life is but a blip on its vast, vast radar. If your life is to matter, it's not going to matter to the universe. It's up to you to make your life matter in the only way you can: by doing things that make a difference to you, to those around you, and to those whose lives you touch. Time is short. You have exactly NOW to do whatever it is you're here to do or to let the inexorable passage of hours and days and years kill your potential like fruit left to die on a vine.

The universe doesn't hate you, but it doesn't love you, either. You're just an atom in its infinite workings. The universe doesn't care if you live, die, suffer, or thrive. Whatever your life here will mean is up to you.

Stop worrying so much about what others think and start being who you're supposed to be. It's time to do some epic shit."

****

This summary was incredible to me. I live stressed to the max because of expectations I put on myself. I don't have enough arms, legs, or brainpower to give one hundred percent to each task because there are too many of them. It gets to the point where I ask, "Why bother? Nothing is going to change. This is the way it is and always will be."

My inner voice stands firm when it says, "That's not true. Things don't have to be this way. I can choose how I act and react."

"Blah, blah, blah," I reply.

But my inner voice speaks the truth. I do have a choice.

Following this reflection, I drew in my sketchbook. I wanted to do something "big."

Some days the "big" might be smaller than others. Still, every effort and step in the right direction is something "big" when it boosts my self-esteem. Each "big" adds up to something great.

I'm not too old to do some epic shit, either. As long as I'm breathing, I can work toward making my dreams come true.

Your Turn

What epic shit do you want to accomplish in your life?

What steps can you take to make your life matter?

More importantly, do you believe you matter? Why? Why not?

What kind of person do you want to be?

Is it realistic?

What's stopping you?

F**k It

My Turn

This entry is a continuation of Why Bother?

In my research for my son's back-to-school books on Amazon, I came across another book that caught my eye called *F**k It* by John C. Parkin.

The following is the book description as copied from Amazon.

****

To say F**k It feels good. To stop struggling and finally do what you wish... to ignore what everyone is telling you and just go your own way... feels really great. In this inspiring and humorous book, John C. Parkin suggests that saying F**k It is the perfect Western expression of the Eastern spiritual concept of letting go, giving up, and finding real freedom by realizing that things don't matter so much (if at all). It's a spiritual way that doesn't require chanting, meditating, or wearing sandals. And it's the very power of this modern-day profanity that makes it perfect for shaking us Westerners out of the stress and anxiety that dominate our daily lives. So, find out how to say F**k It to all your problems and concerns. Say F**k It to all the "shoulds" in your life, and finally do what you want—no matter what other people think!

*****

This reading so inspired me that when I scanned the room and saw dishes in the sink, empty bowls of popcorn my kids left behind, containers of foam stickers my youngest had played with, and dog toys scattered across the rug, I said, "F**k it."

I sat with my sketchbook and drew. My daughter joined me by doing the same in her sketchbook while my younger son worked in a coloring book. In the background, Tim Burton's *A Nightmare Before Christmas* was playing on the television. We sang along and did art.

The dishes, along with everything else, will always be there. I can choose to compulsively clean and do chores when I'm home or say, "F**k it," and ask family members to pitch in so I can enjoy free moments like they do.

Your Turn

What can you say "F**k it" to?

In this regard, I'm not referring to the f**k its we get when ED is in control, and we lose motivation to fight against it.

The f**k its in this activity are things that don't matter or adversely affect us. Gossip, self-pity, and hopelessness negatively affect us and are not options here.

Can you enjoy yourself without caring what others think, provided it isn't harmful to them?

Try it. In your mind, say, "If they don't like it, f**k it."

It's a sense of letting go, and freedom comes with it.

I Think I Can

My Turn

I always tell my kids "can't" isn't a word we use. We must try whatever the task may be. Yet, I resist doing many things and hold off walking through many fears.

Regardless of how hard I try, someone always throws a nail on the road to flatten my tires.

ED thrives on this weakness. It tells me things are too hard to handle, and engaging in behaviors will make dealing with them more manageable. It's the same old lies ED feeds me.

I want an escape from the pressures that face me. They're too big to bear. This overwhelmingness makes me want to scream, "Screw this! Who needs this shit? Run away!"

But where to?

Unfortunately, my problems come with me wherever I go.

I'm supposed to be a role model for my children. Part of that involves coping when life gets tough. When ED tries to suck me back into its deadly web, I have to fight harder to release myself from it.

Saying no to ED should be a no-brainer.

Maybe to somebody not suffering from ED.

It's a daily struggle. ED's been dancing with me for several days, and I'm not letting go of its hand. The result is self-directed anger. Why do I let this happen when I know the outcome?

I have to remind myself that ED is an illness. It will bring me to death if I don't fight against it. It's easy to forget how much ED wants me to disintegrate into nothing. To make my body sick and not treat it like the palace that it is.

My body is the only one I have, and look how I regard it. It's not okay to do this to myself. It's so infuriating!

Your Turn

Are you currently dancing with ED?

How can you dance with recovery instead?

What can you do to break ED's hold on you just for today?

What one thing can you do to treat your body like the palace that it is?

Don't let ED lead the dance with you. Close the moat and lock ED out of your mind, body, and spiritual castle.

ED Is Crying

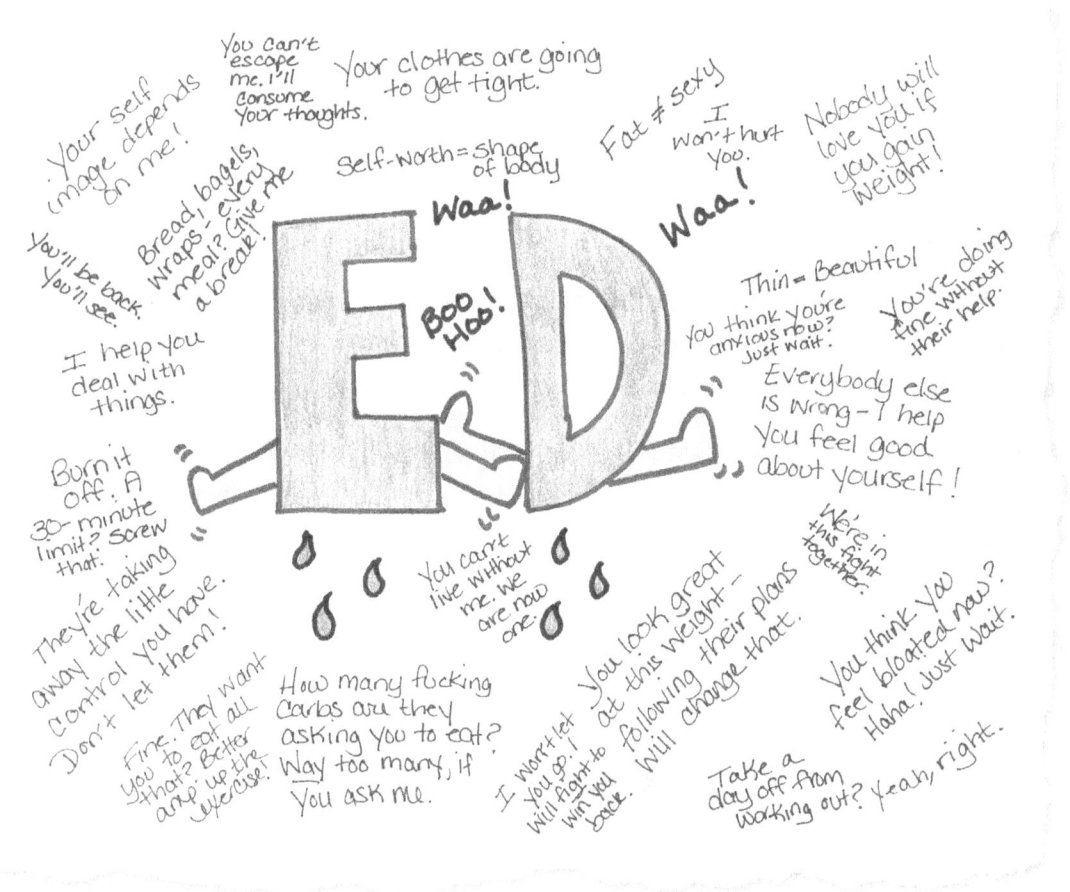

My Turn

ED behaviors discussed. Read with caution.

I had a session with my nutritionist, and my husband joined us. It was so much fun. Not.

The SparkNotes version is I had to sign a 30-day contract to report to her the agreed-upon meal plan daily, take one day off from exercise and limit it to thirty minutes when I engage in it. I must continue to see her weekly. My weight must go up. If these things don't happen in a month, she will release me as a patient and recommend a higher level of care.

I emailed her that I feel others are trying to take something away from me. ED is crying, screaming, kicking, and throwing tantrums. Only reading and sleeping will silence it. It is invading my dreams. It is arguing against the amount of food I'm required to consume. It's telling me if I overeat, I'll gain too much weight.

I'm so tired of this, the fight to eat each meal and snack, and the urge to burn it off with exercise.

The tears won't stop. The inner turmoil and obsession are driving me insane. It's like going through withdrawal, missing my drug of choice.

My ED behaviors are ingrained and have been for years. It's tough to stop a habit, especially one that devised a ridiculous story that it helps me cope with events outside of my being.

ED isn't happy. Faith isn't happy.

My prayer is for my voice to be stronger than ED's because I don't want to go back to treatment. It's going to be a one meal at a time battle for the next month.

Here's to wishing me luck. I'll need it.

Your Turn

Do you find when you stand up to ED, its voice gets raging mad?

How does the turmoil of ED affect your daily life?

Does it affect your relationships? Your job? Your education?

What else does it affect, and how so?

Has anyone given you an ultimatum about recovering from ED or having consequences?

If so, has there been a follow-through?

Let's Make A Deal

My Turn

In trying to silence my ED voice, who won't give it a rest for a second, I caved in and made a deal with it. In my eating disorder support group, I've heard that ED will always be waiting on the sidelines if I want to join forces with it again. I can try something different, and if I don't like the results, I can go back to it.

Keeping this idea in mind, I'm mentally debating the argument to give the nutritionist her thirty-days ultimatum (ED Is Crying entry). If I'm not feeling better at the end of the four weeks, ED will be waiting with open arms, and we can reunite.

My hope is that the new changes I'm making will become more habitual, become something I can live with, and quiet ED's voice the more I go against its wishes.

I'm sure it will be a Pay-Per-View fight worth watching because I honestly can't predict who the winner will be. Again, it's going to be one meal, one snack at a time. Otherwise, the entire process will be too much to take on.

Just for today, I will try to do the right thing. Actually, just for this minute, I will try to do the right thing.

Your Turn

What are your thoughts about making a deal with ED?

What if you were to tell ED you're going to try recovery for thirty days, and after that if you aren't happy, you can go back to it?

Not to worry, ED will happily take you back.

Why not try something new?

You already know what it's like to live with ED. It sucks.

You might get a glimpse of recovery and decide to stick with it. I've been up and down in it. My experience has been that the serenity of recovery far outweighs the misery of ED.

Section III
Living In The Now

NOW

My Turn

I can compare my life to a classroom. My classwork, homework, and life work require reinforcement because I quickly forget the lessons and assignments even though the instructions are clear.

My current discipline policy has been one of self-criticism. Detentions, referrals, and suspensions are useless. My thoughts are punishment enough.

My daily assignments are tools for the changes I'm seeking as life unveils itself. Many lessons could use further explanation, even tutoring, because I have trouble grasping and retaining them the first, second, and even third time learning them.

There are moments when I'm just not in the right mindset to learn something new, or the timing is off, and I'm not open to its presentation.

Life always has a way of sneaking the same lessons into the mix so that at some point, I'll be present and get the message. I can be stubborn and thick-headed when I want to be.

Recovery from my eating disorder has been one area where I'd prefer to remain outside the classroom. There's too much to learn, study, and recite. Forget that.

However, I'm now on the inside, asking questions and relying on others in recovery for guidance. I need their knowledge and understanding. I can't do it alone, even though ED tells me I can, without any assistance.

Lessons are flying at me from all sides. It can be both confusing and overwhelming, not to mention terrifying.

There are many mornings I want to skip "life school" because hearing the information taught sounds easy, but doing the actual footwork and practicing the skills are like walking through quicksand.

This entry brings to mind a spiral-bound notebook I purchased for my daughter. The cover reads, "Dear Math, I am not a psychiatrist. Please solve your own problems."

The quote makes me smile because, in so many ways, it represents how I feel.

Recovery can be like sitting in a trigonometry class when I don't know basic addition. I understand the suggestions made when my therapist or nutritionist poses them, but when push comes to shove, and I have to practice the tasks in real life, my automatic response is, "I can't do this. It's too hard."

Like anything else, especially math, since it's my worst subject, the more I practice something, the easier it becomes.

Math has never been my forte, but I know recovery has to be, so skipping homework assignments isn't an option. It's a must, or else I will fail. And failure in eating disorder recovery ultimately leads to death. With that scary reality in mind, I am motivated to *attempt* the asinine trig problems. I say this with irritation because all the work necessary for recovery can be disheartening.

The subjects I must study, and practice are:

Counting my blessings—I am grateful to say there are many.

Stopping and smelling the roses—not literally since I'm allergic to them.

Learning from and not repeating past mistakes. But when I do, it's not okay to criticize myself.

Filling my life with art, writing, and music.

Practicing these lessons **daily**.

An integral part of being in the classroom of life is to show up. I can't afford to be absent or daydream because I might just miss the most important lesson I'm supposed to learn.

Your Turn

How will you be present in your life today? I mean *really* be present, not just go through the motions.

What one subject requires special attention and possible tutoring?

You can make up your own subjects. You don't have to use mine. In this class, there are no wrong answers, and you get praise for effort. Even if you make a mistake, as long as you pick up the pencil and try to solve the problem again, you earn a reward.

The pencils we use don't have erasers, which translates to the worst mistakes can lead to the best learning.

Effort is paramount. Life is the teacher. You are the student. You give the grades.

Please don't be a nasty teacher who doesn't grade on the curve or give credit for attempts. Be kind to yourself. Picture a sweet and loving kindergarten teacher who is gentle and nurturing with new students entering "real" school and leaving their parents. It can be scary, let alone an adjustment. Be that caring kindergarten teacher because similar to those five and six-year-olds, we, too, are adjusting to change. In our case, it's recovery.

In The Moment

My Turn

I'm getting waves of calmness and am more at ease. It scares me because I know the meek, do-it-all behaviors and thoughts are lurking in the bushes behind me. I am petrified they'll seize hold of me again.

Recovery is scary.

I'm so used to feeling anxious that when I'm in a peaceful frame of mind—yes, I've been there—I somehow sabotage myself by allowing ED to threaten me.

It's vital not to forget ED's presence, so it doesn't sneak up on me unexpectedly, and BAM! put me back under its spell.

I can't allow myself to avoid living in the present because of my fear of the past.

There's an expression that reads: yesterday is history; tomorrow is a mystery; today is a gift. That's why it's called the present. When we stop and think about it, isn't the present all we have?

Your Turn

What can you do to immerse yourself fully in the present moment?

I have found that merely giving my children or husband a hug or playing with my dogs can snap me back into the moment and put a smile on my face.

Enjoy these gifts.

We can't let past upsets engulf us and bring us back to our eating disorders' uncomfortable comfort. It's a misperception.

Who enjoys serving an anxiety-filled life sentence in their head?

I don't.

Don't waste a minute. Each one is all we have. Be truly present in it.

*****

Add-on during editing.

Breathe.

Place your hand on your chest and feel your heartbeat. Say thank you for all your heart is doing despite the abuse we put our bodies through.

Experience the rush of fresh air as it fills your lungs.

The warmth of the exhale.

Just be with your breath.

Watch a video of babies laughing or puppies being silly.

Smell your favorite essential oil.

Read an inspirational message.

Read jokes on Pinterest (a personal favorite to lighten my mood).

Appreciate the love you have in your heart for another person. Let that abundance fill you. Now flip it around and give it to yourself. It's been easier to give mine to others. It's something I'm working hard to change.

Just be present. No past. No future.

Permit yourself to be in the here and now without remnants of the past or worries about the future. It makes a difference with practice.

Stress = I'm Not Hungry

My Turn

Here's a practical coping strategy I picked up along the line. When confronted with stress, my stomach feels full, and I tell others to leave me alone. When in reality, I'm lonely in my isolation and am starving for attention.

I'm not one to share my inner thoughts. I prefer to hide them. I'm like a human Build-A-Bear with stuffing oozing out from all sides, trying to free itself.

Sadness and anger prefer to stay buried. They settle in my belly, causing the fullness I'm referring to. When these emotions fill me, hunger cues go out the window. Hence, I don't "feel" hungry.

Your Turn

What are your coping mechanisms for dealing with stress?

List the negative ones.

Hint: ED goes on this list, even though it will argue against it.

What are positive coping mechanisms aiding in your recovery?

I discovered I have a lot of winners in my recovery box. They include:

Using my voice assertively (not easy by any stretch of the imagination).

Drawing to express my feelings.

Working with and not against my team's suggestions.

Going to my support group when necessary.

Structuring my time.

Allowing myself to make mistakes.

Meditating.

Creative writing.

Pleasure reading.

Doing things I enjoy like alternative therapies.

Balancing work and play.

The list continues to grow. Some tools have always been in my box, but I forget to use them or misuse them.

****

Add-on during editing.

If you can't think of a positive coping mechanism and your brain won't cooperate, something we all encounter, try to STOP and go within.

Take a pause.

Check-in with yourself.

What's going on around you?

What's going on inside you (emotionally)?

Is the situation something you can control? If it isn't, let it go.

If you can change it, what can you do to make it better?

If possible, go outside and soak up the peacefulness of nature.

Allow the air to hug you.

Breathe in the scents.

Touch a piece of grass or examine the details on a leaf.

Watch a butterfly dance over a flower.

Listen to birds chirping.

What designs do you see in the clouds?

How does the temperature feel against your skin?

Look at the root system of a tree. Some are pretty amazing.

Put a lost earthworm in the grass. I will usually use cardboard or something in recycling to save a worm because I'm not particularly fond of touching critters.

A simple exercise like this can lighten the darkness in our minds.

Why not try it out? There are so many extraordinary sights to see when we open our eyes, truly open them, and live in the moment.

Where's Me Time?

My Turn

During treatment, I learned how I neglected my mind, body, and spirit. There's always a reason or excuse for not taking care of myself.

Nobody will give me that time. It's a conscious choice to give it to myself, and not doing so isn't an option.

Balance is necessary for living a healthy life. But how can I create balance when one side of my seesaw is filled with everyone else's needs while mine remains empty?

The answer is to add things to my side that uplift and make me feel better, and more importantly, provide me with a sense of worthiness. It goes back to self-care.

Your Turn

How can you balance your seesaw?

What can you do to keep it level?

Imagine the little bubble that floats to one side when a car seat or leveler is unbalanced. The bubble represents our mental status. When we are out of alignment, it shifts to one side, which makes us tip over, fall, and get hurt. Haven't we been hurt enough?

I have, and I'm tired of wearing Band-Aids from head to toe to cover up my bruises.

****

Add-on during editing (written during the COVID pandemic quarantine).

My mind automatically reverts to negative thinking. I wake up worried about all the tasks I have to accomplish. If I don't center myself when I wake up, I start the day filled with anxiety.

Pause.

I'm taking a deep breath as I write this because merely thinking about my responsibilities creates tension.

In a sense, I have to brainwash my mind to think positive thoughts. It isn't instinctive. When in a slump, which I'm currently in, I kick up my self-care routine.

This is what I'm doing:

Meditating.

Listening to inspirational speakers on YouTube.

Attending my Codependency Anonymous meetings via Zoom.

Editing my romance novels.

Doing these activities helps me refocus and change my perspective.

I am attending a Mindfulness/Happiness workshop, and the teacher had us repeat the mantra: *I have enough. I do enough. I am enough.*

I have enough.

When I break it down, I have everything I need. Sure, we all have wants, but for the most part, my needs are met. I practice using my voice when they're not.

I do enough.

I don't have to rationalize or make excuses for my decisions. As long as I'm not hurting or neglecting others, it's not my problem if they disagree with my choices.

I'm spending a good chunk of time on different mindfulness activities. In the past, I would have felt guilty for taking "me" time. No longer. Self-care is my medicine; it helps keep me grounded.

I am enough.

The teacher in our class mentioned that we could be having a wonderful day, but if someone rolls their eyes at us, that's what we will fixate on.

I identified with this. Heaven forbid someone gets upset with me. I know this comes from my abandonment issues. The bottom line is, I won't please everyone, and expecting to do so is unrealistic. And if someone did roll their eyes at me, it's more about that person than it is me. That's not to say I won't give it airtime in my head, but I no longer fixate on others' issues, nor do I want negative people in my life.

Time To Walk

My Turn

Doing the resentment package in treatment was an eye-opener. I have written my dad multiple letters in the past, which I never gave to him. I have talked endlessly about my childhood during therapy sessions.

For some reason, I finally felt I was at a place to let my anger toward him go. What's done is done.

Letting go of resentments is paramount if I want to heal.

It is from changing my viewpoint that I've realized I deserve respect and will accept nothing less. I am no longer a doormat for others to walk over.

From these changes in perspective, I have gained acceptance, compassion, and empathy toward my dad, who has the beginning stages of Alzheimer's. It's a horrible disease to witness.

When I see my father, I sense a kind man with a loving heart. He found his inner truth and became enlightened, someone to admire. He accepts the cards life has dealt him and continues to seek inner peace and guidance. I strive for what he has found.

Your Turn

Write down your resentments.

Now toss them in the trash. Rip them to shreds. Burn them. Stomp on them. Flush them down the toilet.

They serve no purpose and only agonize us.

Acknowledging abuse and insults from others doesn't mean we accept unacceptable behavior, nor does it mean injustices are justified. They aren't. It means we must liberate ourselves from their hold on us.

As adults, we are the only ones who can stop others from harming us emotionally, physically, and spiritually.

Haven't we suffered enough at the wrongdoing of others?

Freeing ourselves from these deep wounds brings us to the acceptance of what is.

****

Add-on during editing.

The past is what it is. We can change our reactions and thoughts about it, though, so it no longer has to consume us. It has taken me years to find forgiveness for the emotional abuse I suffered as a child from my father's angry outbursts.

Even now, loud, argumentative voices startle me and revert me to my childhood of uncertainty. If possible, I physically remove myself and rephrase my self-talk if the anger is directed at someone else. If it's aimed at me, I'll ask the person to speak in a different tone of voice. If the person isn't willing to,

I'll state that I'll continue the conversation when they are—no ifs, ands, or buts about it. My voice has gained strength in this area, and it's gratifying to stand up for myself.

You can stand up for yourself, too. It takes effort. But you deserve the respect you ask for. We all do.

Section IV
Mental Circles

Mental Merry-Go-Round

My Turn

I'm like a hamster running in circles inside a wheel going nowhere. The ride never ends, and I'm exhausted. The insanity is it's so easy to stop the spinning wheel. All I have to do is hop off.

I've become so accustomed to chasing my tail that merely considering stopping the cycle of insanity can feel as extreme and intense as jumping off a tall cliff into an unknown abyss with no safety net in sight.

Recovery is blind faith. It's jumping off that cliff into mysterious and unfamiliar territory.

My mind tells me it's better to keep running in circles than try something new, even if it's good for me. My irrational thoughts convince me to continue these tiresome patterns.

The screaming of my recovery voice is a loud reprimand. I can't wait until it becomes a quiet and gentle reminder.

All I know is the Habitrail I'm currently on has left me dizzy, tired, and in desperate need of a break. It's high time I climb off and sit on the bench to take a well-deserved rest.

Your Turn

What can you do to get off the Mental Merry-Go-Round—the spinning, repetitive thoughts that keep you stuck in a tormented mindset?

Make a to-do list, even if there's only one item, of tools you can use to get off the ride and join me on the bench.

The items might include:

Texting a friend who can offer encouragement.

Hugging a loved one.

Listening and singing along to a favorite song.

Meditating.

Journaling.

Praying.

Cuddling with a pet or stuffed animal (I'm guilty of snuggling with a plush).

Getting fresh air.

Observing the beauty of nature.

Taking a bubble bath.

Pleasure reading.

Meeting up with a friend or loved one and sharing your feelings (scary stuff!).

The possibilities are endless. I know I repeat the same suggestions often. It's because they have been so helpful in my recovery.

You can choose anything which jams the switch on the Merry-Go-Round, even if only temporarily.

ED encourages us to hold its hand so we can better deal with stress and overwhelming emotions. It might even be on a subconscious level, an automatic response to a trigger or event.

It's WRONG.

Awareness will start to settle in and arm us to act instead of succumbing to ED's wishes, but we must sit on the bench and give ourselves a break.

Watch Out! She's Going To Blow!

My Turn

I have a slew of feelings. I opened up and shared about them during our treatment group, but they often get so intense it becomes unbearable.

Instead of acting out on ED behaviors, I chose to distract myself by drawing, and to my surprise, it offered some relief.

There are many occasions when I feel like my head is going to blow off my body with steam shooting out of both ears, similar to what you might see on an old cartoon.

When that happens, daily expectations become too challenging to handle. The sad reality is that I'm the one who puts high expectations and deadlines on myself.

Specific tasks must get done, such as getting my kids to school, taking care of the dogs, my job, etc. However, many others aren't as important as I make them out to be. In my eyes, every item on my list has equal importance. Logically, that can't be the case.

I use an old-fashioned planner, not my smartphone, to list my daily and weekly obligations. I prefer to look at my week in advance for organizational purposes, weeding out scheduling conflicts, and fitting in self-care.

My worrisome thoughts send me into a tailspin. I expect to accomplish an entire week's worth of responsibilities in a few short hours, which leads to mental and physical exhaustion.

And then there is the buying and returning routine. This behavior is another distraction I've added to my unhealthy coping basket. In this undertaking, I purchase items on sale, which gives me a high, then experience guilt, which leads me to "purge," if you will, by returning them.

My time is worth more than busying myself with menial tasks as a means to escape underlying feelings.

Listing the importance of my duties makes a difference. I sort them into musts, shoulds (not emergent), and optional. For example, cleaning the tops of my kitchen cabinets is optional.

The priority is the musts. The rest can wait. Looking at the items in terms of value gives me a better handle over accomplishing them without stretching myself too thin.

Your Turn

What's on your to-do list?

What must be done?

What should be done but can realistically wait, meaning it's not the end of the world if it doesn't get done this instant?

My example of cleaning the tops of the kitchen cabinets comes to mind here.

What "me" time will you schedule in?

This task isn't an option. It should be number one every day.

Begin to prioritize your responsibilities, and by all means, ask for help. I rarely do and, as a result, get overwhelmed.

Too Much

My Turn

I'm not doing well. I have no energy or desire to do anything, nada—which translates to nothing. My kids and work are suffocating me, and I lack adult stimulation. There is always something to do, and I'm not taking breaks to play, draw, or participate in things I enjoy. There's no "me" time.

The result is an "I don't care" attitude or the "f**k its," as my support group likes to call it. Either way, this mindset delights ED and brings it into full swing.

During the beginning of my recovery journey, I would usually let ED win because the alternative was too scary to consider. I know this might sound irrational to an outsider, but it's logical to someone suffering from an eating disorder. At least to me, it is.

There were periods I wasn't motivated to do the necessary footwork because it was too daunting.

****

Add-on during editing.

When I get into these slumps, I kick up my efforts. I'll text a friend, schedule visits with my nutritionist closer together, keep my therapy appointments steady, meditate more, watch inspirational videos on YouTube, and write.

Being in the "everything is too much" mindset sucks. There's no better way to describe it. The thing is, everyone has ups and downs, not just us. Others only deal with their downs differently than we do.

I am first learning as an adult how to handle life on life's terms. It's not fun by any means. I would have preferred to learn these skills early on when I was a child, but that wasn't the case. Fortunately, it's never too late to try recovery and live a productive and happy life.

Change can and does happen, but it's up to us to be willing to take that initial step. If I'm not open-minded, it wouldn't matter if I saw my nutritionist daily or had five hours of therapy. Everything would remain status quo.

Your Turn

What do you do when life feels like it's too much to handle?

Does your eating disorder thrive on those days?

Mine does.

Being conscious when these slumps hit me gives me ammunition to fight against them. I don't always win, but at least I have a choice. I have found that when I make poor ones, my thoughts only beat me up more.

It isn't unheard of for awareness to feel like our worst enemy, but ironically, it's the opposite. It's our healthy voices trying to regain power from the grips of ED. Listen to that voice.

I am grateful to have experienced glimpses of inner peace from doing the right thing and taking care of myself. I want more from where that is coming, which motivates me to listen to my healthy voice faster than I used to.

Cycles Of Trouble

My Turn

The cycles that could lead to trouble.

When my anxiety level rises, I become acutely in tune with the behaviors I engage in to ease it. The patterns are crystal clear.

One of the favorites that I've mentioned is buying things, letting guilt set in, and then returning them. While at the shop, I'll see new stuff, buy it, and there I go again, off to the races. It's a never-ending cycle until I stop it.

These cycles also include cleaning frenzies of closets, drawers, cabinets, and the list continues. It is spellbinding because I go from one task to the next to quell my inner stress, oblivious about my actions.

Being watchful of these cycles has enabled me to stop and ask, "What is going on?"

Usually, I'm neglecting or putting too much pressure on myself in some area of my life. Going underneath the anxiety or fear where my primary feelings reside is where the truth lies.

Your Turn

Do you find if you get hold of one area in recovery, unhealthy behaviors creep into other areas?

What are your cycles or patterns?

Ask yourself, "What's going on that's making me act out?"

Dig deep. Journal. Talk to your therapist or a trusted friend.

My experience has shown that ignoring pain causes it to worsen.

The only way to stop negative cycles or patterns is first to recognize them—awareness. Then and only then can we see how unmanageable they make our lives, just like ED does.

Magnifying Glass

My Turn

Act and not react is a concept I learned long ago from attending Twelve-Step groups.

It's easy to react to stressors that bombard me daily. A perfect example is a scenario that happened this morning. My mom is in the hospital with internal bleeding. I'm consciously trying to remain present by gaining information from the doctors before freaking out, my usual style, especially when it comes to my mother and sickness.

I told my daughter about her grandma, and her immediate response was, "Is she going to die?"

I wonder who she learned reactionary behavior from. I say this with a sarcastic tone.

We discussed my drawing, which she saw me working on a few nights prior.

Looking at life through a magnifying glass makes everything more enormous and catastrophic than it is. I can be confronted with a situation and play out all the horrible outcomes that might result from it. This behavior has a place to be warranted. When it affects my ability to function and causes debilitating anxiety, it's not, and I need to remove the magnifying glass and put it back in my youngest son's toy bin.

Little things should remain just that, little.

Your Turn

Are you magnifying any situations in your life?

What are they?

What would they look like if you removed the magnifying glass?

Are they as overwhelming?

If so, what if you imagined putting on special glasses that shrank the severity of them?

Would it be easier to handle them by seeing them for what they are, with a fresh perspective?

Once we get a clearer picture of something, it's easier to develop a game plan and face it. Also, viewing it as smaller than it is can make it less daunting to confront.

As an aside, my mom was okay and got released from the hospital within the week.

Running On Empty

My Turn

ED behaviors discussed. Read with caution.

I went back to my support group after taking a break for a few months. I go through periods when attending does more harm than good.

The predominant theme was one I'm already familiar with—over-giving to others.

My husband always hears me say I feel drained, and there's nothing left for me to give. Despite this, those around me still demand more. I won't say no and put everyone else in front of the line.

I have made many excuses for not working on my romance books, which fill me and ignite my inner light.

Once again, I'm telling myself certain things can wait and using the "F**k it" technique described in the F**k It entry.

My husband and I ran errands kid-free. He suggested we go to lunch, to which I replied, "I'm not hungry."

Within a half-hour, I ate the snack stored in my purse. My husband asked why I was eating when I said no to lunch. I'll usually come up with an excuse to protect ED, but I didn't, choosing instead to tell him the truth. We had plans to go out to dinner with his parents, and it would be too much food to consume in one day. So said ED.

My husband looked at me in shock. It snapped me into reality, angering me because I saw how ED was manipulating me.

The situation was an eye-opener. I was plugged into ED's influence yet went against its wishes. My husband and I went to lunch and then to dinner as planned. I will add ED kept reminding me that I had overeaten. I consciously ignored it.

The up and down road of recovery is precisely that. I reflect on the beginning of my journey, and there have been great strides. I'm patting myself on the back for these steps forward.

Your Turn

Have you made any encouraging changes that you can applaud yourself for?

Praising ourselves is necessary. It's like punching ED in the face—a double bonus.

Saying there haven't been any doesn't cut it. Reading this journal entry counts as self-care and deserves praise.

Keep in mind that small things we overlook as insignificant could be major recovery milestones.

It's Always The Same

My Turn

We spoke about the rules we live by in my support group. When I contemplate this, I can see the mental hell I put myself through because of my rules—the constraints I've created throughout my life that affect every action I take.

When I listen to the list of rules in my head, it's no wonder I live with such an inordinate amount of anxiety. I give myself timelines for getting things done, what and how much I'm allowed to eat, the amount of cleaning I should do daily, task after task.

Sure, in the real world, there are deadlines. I'm not referring to these. I'm talking about the unrealistic deadlines I put on myself.

Why does everything have to be done right now?

I got a new therapist. I was stagnant. It wasn't an easy decision to make, and I delayed it for quite a while because transitions involve change—a word ED hates.

Change can be the perfect catalyst to reignite the fires within.

After two visits, my new therapist mentioned that I frequently engage in activities to avoid feeling. I already knew this about myself but was keen on her insight.

The only person who cuts in line at the rule-changing counter and takes my turn is ED, who files a complaint about allowing returns or exchanges on rules.

Fear of rejection, abandonment, being imperfect, yada yada, keep me standing in line, waiting to argue against ED's grievance with the rule-changing policy.

Your Turn

What are your rules?

How and why did you come up with them?

The answer might take a bit of digging.

Fear underlies many, if not all, of our rules. What are your fears?

Do you believe unfavorable rules are exchangeable for new ones?

At times, my thoughts are loud and dictate how I should live, act, and react. Things are slowly changing.

What one conscious choice can you make to do something different from the norm? It can be anything.

What one destructive rule that you follow can you trash?

It doesn't have to be permanent. Try it out for good measure. It might cause stress afterward, but the challenge will hopefully be rewarding enough to override the angst.

Drowning

My Turn

ED behaviors discussed. Read with caution.

Here I am, almost two years into recovery, and I'm still fighting against ED.

Have changes been made? Yes.

Do I still hold on to "safe" foods, as ED likes to call them? Yes.

The topic of deserving came up in my support group.

It's easy to talk about deserving things but believing it is a different story altogether.

I have yet to do away with the burden of overextending myself. ED has become a subconscious coping strategy. It's a means to punish myself for being easily overwhelmed by the pressure I put on myself.

Thoughts of "This is too much to handle" and "I can't take it anymore" surface. I internalize this frustration because using my voice is so hard.

This internal dialogue manifests itself physically because the underlying feelings have to be dealt with and released. The resulting anxiety makes me want to exercise to rid of it and restrict my eating. The worst part is nothing gets better after giving in to ED's demands other than more self-criticism.

It becomes a revolving door of thoughts/behaviors/self-punishment.

The question remains: Who, other than myself, tells me I don't deserve to be happy?

My therapist and I spoke about whether my feelings match my rational thoughts. They don't. They actually conflict, which results in agitation. She suggested I journal since I have difficulty sharing with others. I end up stuffing all week until our next visit or my session with my nutritionist. Journaling can also be done after eating suggested foods on my meal plan to ease the distress of engaging in "unsafe" meals—according to ED.

Usually, when I eat a recommended meal, I'll tell myself I'll remain full until the next one. As if I can control my body's demand for food. ED thinks it can.

Will doing this homework mean I've been struck by the Deserving Lightning Rod?

No.

But maybe if I do it regularly, it will spark the revelation that I deserve to live a life better than the one ED wants for me.

Your Turn

Do you believe you deserve to recover?

If yes, hurray for you, and I mean that wholeheartedly.

If not, what will it take to come to terms with the *fact* that you deserve happiness and recovery?

What can you do to stop ED's chatter in between and during meals?

Can you write or share before, during, or after meals to release unease?

If eating a prescribed meal seems impossible, and you are alone, can you video chat or call someone to support you through it and afterward?

If you aren't alone, can you ask a family member, friend, or partner you trust to sit with you?

Can you take a picture both before and after a meal and send it to a trusted source for accountability?

ED despises accountability.

I have mastered eating incognito so that nobody knows what or how much I've eaten. My healthy voice understands that accountability is annoying but essential to fighting against ED.

When we lie to others about our engagement with ED, we are only hurting ourselves, and eventually, that guilt eats at us.

The Bench

My Turn

My therapist suggested I try EMDR (Eye Movement Desensitization and Reprocessing) to deal with my PTSD. I didn't know what to expect. It was similar to hypnosis. In my mind, I went to my safe place at the beach, where I sat on a rocking chair with my feet pressed into the warm sand and a cool breeze blowing against my skin.

What I didn't expect was for Christian Grey to show up. How odd. Or was it?

Mr. Grey had been a tremendous resource during treatment and times of stress, sucking me out of my world and into his.

During the session, he served as my protector, symbolizing my yearning for security. Alexandra made an appearance as well, dancing gracefully as always.

While relishing the serene atmosphere, I suddenly yelled, "F**k you!" but nobody was around me.

Who was I speaking to?

I realized I aimed the words at myself.

When I tried to reel Alexandra in, I couldn't. It became a wrestling match between us. Her on top of me, pinning me down, and me fighting against her by not allowing her to return home. Why was I attacking her when she is such a beautiful part of me?

Finally, Christian, Alexandra, and I sat on a bench, the three of us staring at the ocean.

After the session, I left with sadness over how my early life experiences created the bundle of nerves I am today. I've convinced myself I'm passive. The therapist disagreed, arguing I allow myself to be because I don't use my voice.

As long as I keep *doing* instead of *being*, ED will remain by my side.

Avoidance. It's a word I know well.

Your Turn

How does it feel to live with ED?

Is there self-blame for having ED?

Is there shame?

Are you compassionate with yourself, or do you speak to yourself harshly?

Do you feel stuck, unable to move forward?

What would have to change in your thinking and behavior for you to get unstuck?

How can you act upon the changes you reflected on above?

Start with one act. Babies don't go from crawling to running. They take a step, fall. Take two steps, fall.

It's the same with recovery. A step. A fall. Get up.

Section V
Wearing A Mask

Perceptions Are Deceiving

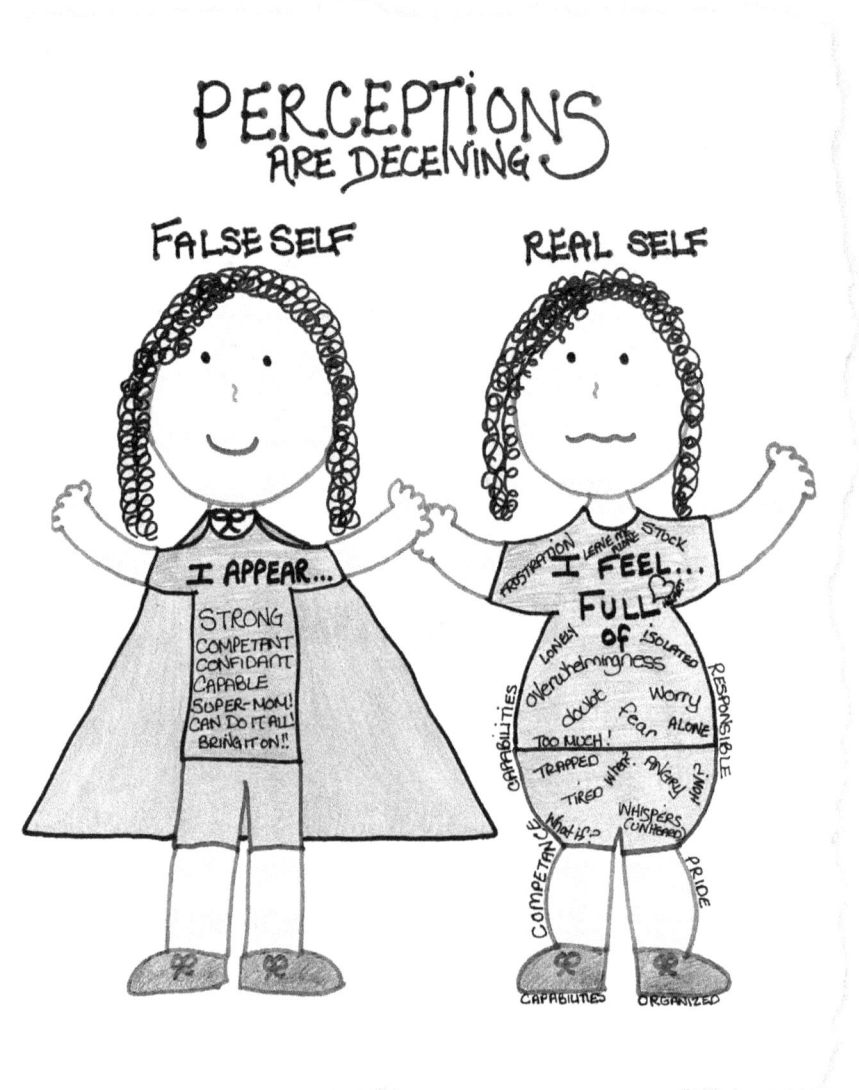

My Turn

To the outside world I present myself as strong and capable. Both of which I'll proudly admit to being. But if I genuinely have these traits, why am I so full of self-doubt?

This insecurity makes me feel "full." It's no wonder I have no appetite.

Self-defeating thoughts consume me to the extent there isn't much space left for anything else, especially the fun stuff, which will make me hungry for life.

My false self wears a cape. She's a superwoman who can do it all, unfazed by the battles she faces daily while appearing calm and collected.

Little does the outside world know the cape hides the truth.

What I *believe* to be my true self and what I *know* to be my true self are two separate entities.

I have a distorted self-perception. I can logically admit I am competent and intelligent. I prove it to myself daily. However, my mind tells me otherwise. It tells me I am neither of these things. That I don't have choices and that this is the way things are and shall remain. It tells me I can handle life's challenges better with ED and Audrey holding my hands.

I can't wait until my real self—the one filled with pride, knowledge, confidence, compassion, empathy, and love—reveals herself to the world so my false self can kiss its ass goodbye. My natural capabilities will then shine from the inside out. That is the authentic me I want to believe in and know harmoniously.

Your Turn

Are you wearing a cape to hide the real you?

Who is the real you (a loaded question)?

Who is the false you that you present to the world?

How can you get rid of the cape to allow the real you to shine through and present itself?

I'm not asking for miracles as I'm right here on this journey with you. All I'm asking is for you to untie one string of the cape to let the person you are have permission to reveal itself.

Explore these thoughts. Reflect on them. See what comes up. Journal if you so desire.

I say to explore and reflect because it's easy to give one-word responses. The real work comes from going within.

****

Add-on during editing.

My current therapist loves to tell me to "go deeper." It drives me mad. But, when I dig below the surface, I gain more insight into the real issues at hand.

When I'm upset, I tell myself to go deeper. It usually boils down to a need being unmet. I delve more into this in the Seesaw Of Needs entry.

She has suggested this technique so often it has become routine. It's been an excellent tool to help me get to the root of my struggles. Maybe it can help you, too.

Feeling Lonely

How is it that I feel lonely?

My Turn

I have a full house—three kids, two dogs, and a caring husband. There is always something going on, yet I'm lonely, disconnected, and stuck in my head. I haven't found where this loneliness stems from.

****

Add-on during editing.

Loneliness is something I still encounter. I can be in a room full of people and feel alone. There is a wall around my heart that protects it from getting hurt. It has suffered a lifetime of pain. My motivation to let people in is next to nothing.

The only outsiders I freely open up to are the women in my Codependency Anonymous group and other support groups because the attendees relate and accept me. Others are far and few between.

Worthiness is territory I continue to develop. Rewiring my brain is ongoing. Developing self-acceptance is a full-time job.

I add in newer entries to demonstrate how recovery is continuous. Some areas have improved, whereas others require more concentration. The difference today is I'm okay with it. I don't have to beat myself up for being flawed. We all are. Perfection doesn't exist. I have come to terms with this truth and have stopped trying to achieve the unobtainable.

Your Turn

Do you feel disconnected from others?

If so, how do you reconnect?

When you do, does the loneliness vanish?

What would it take to make the loneliness disappear?

****

Add-on during editing.

As I mentioned, loneliness still resides within me. That's not to say I'm not better able to connect with others, which comes from being more spiritually sound and accepting of myself. I'm attracted to like-minded people and less drawn to those who need saving.

Gray Skies

My Turn

I always go out wearing a smile, even if I'm crying inside. People have made comments that I'm mellow and chill. Ha-ha! If they only knew.

My husband and oldest son had a "moment," and it was a doozy. My instinct as a mother was to stop their verbal sparring. Mind you, my older son has no problem using his voice and speaking his mind.

During their argument, many emotions were flying. Coming from a childhood where angry outbursts came out of nowhere, their raised voices set off a panic reaction. It's instinctual, an automatic response from my traumatic past. I had a sense that I was out of my body, disassociation, if you will.

Afterward, my husband was upset at me for not taking his side.

Directly following the incident, my younger son asked me to take him outside to play freeze tag. My heart was racing a mile a minute. Regardless, I remained calm when I addressed him.

The first thought that popped into my mind was to act out. ED took my vulnerability as the perfect opportunity to catch me when I was off-guard.

I told my younger son I would play with him in a little while because I needed a time out. I grabbed my phone, put on Loverboy, and took a peaceful walk, craving space and fresh air.

The ED thoughts lessened.

When I got home, I wondered how I could put my angst into a drawing.

At my support group, we spoke about sitting with our feelings instead of running from them by acting out with ED. As I write, I'm sitting with unpleasant ones. It sucks, but I know it's the right thing to do.

To be honest, at the moment, I don't want to wear a pretend happy face or smile—things that serve ED. Doing so makes others think everything is fine in Faith World.

If I wore expressions that matched my moods, it would allow others to lend a hand without asking what's wrong, which would only enable me to silence my voice.

With recovery comes clarity. It's magical.

And in case you were wondering, I didn't forget to play freeze tag with my son. It was fun.

Your Turn

Do you wear a happy face and pretend everything is okay?

When is it appropriate to take it off?

With whom do you feel it is appropriate to take it off?

What do you do with your feelings when you don't want to share them?

If you are in a rut, write some options to pick from so you can sit with the discomfort.

Crappy moods don't have to be isolating. Tools can include reaching out to another person, journaling, meditating, coloring, or doodling. Anything that allows you to sit with restlessness and apprehension without turning to ED can be one.

Regarding tools, consider ED to be an ax. It doesn't belong or fit inside your box. Besides, it only wants to butcher you into a million pieces anyway, so why would you include it?

Yes, this is a disturbing metaphor, but it speaks the truth. We have to view ED for what it is: a murderer.

Ouch!

My Turn

I'm sensitive to even the slightest thing, my feelings easily hurt, and I dare not use my voice in case I insult someone.

Many aren't aware that my destiny was to become the world's therapist, one who can solve everybody's problems, except my own. At least, that's the burden I carry by having a codependent personality.

I've always been a fixer, a Bob the Builder of people's emotions. Well, guess what? I could use some fixing myself.

It goes back to the simple concept of using my voice and being heard. Words remain at the base of my throat. They literally won't come out of my mouth.

Fearing an angry reaction from others is why they get stuck. I would rather keep my mouth shut to avoid a possible confrontation. Unfortunately, not voicing my opinions comes at the expense of my emotional health. I end up getting taken advantage of and frustrated in return.

Recovery is about self-care. Giving it to myself doesn't happen as regularly as it should, and this is a *definite* should. Ever the people-pleaser, this has been an onerous barrier to cross.

My mother always told me that the first no is the hardest, but it must be said, even if others get insulted. Yessing everyone leads to overwhelm. Taking on someone else's stuff is where I have to draw the line.

Recovery isn't a miracle cure where everything becomes easy-peasy, and I dance on air. It's about healing myself because, contrary to my belief, I don't have superhuman powers to make everybody and their mother feel better. Sure, I can be supportive as long as I don't lose myself in the process.

Setting boundaries with those who trigger me or stifle my growth is another must.

My goals in recovery are few but speak a thousand words:

To be comfortable in my skin.

To speak my mind without fearing the consequences that follow.

To take care of my needs first (this is *not* selfish).

To listen to my body's signals when enough is enough instead of pushing myself to the brink of exhaustion.

To learn to say no.

To have balance and peace.

To accept the things I can't control.

To live in the moment.

To have fun.

To be gentle with myself.

To face my fears.

To reach out for support.

To connect with others.

To set boundaries, as mentioned above.

To be *in*dependent rather than *co*dependent.

Your Turn

What are you doing to take care of yourself?

What and who can you say no to?

Who do you have difficulty saying no to? Why?

What would give you the courage to speak your truth in an assertive, non-aggressive manner?

I am a firm believer that it's not *what* you say but *how* you say it.

What are your goals in recovery?

Make them realistic.

Wishing traumatic pasts didn't happen or that everything will turn up rainbows and unicorns isn't possible. Life is still life. We have to learn how to live it with healthier coping mechanisms, i.e., tools for success.

Digging For Feelings

My Turn

During therapy, I love to chat about every aspect of my life, except what's going on beneath the surface.

My therapist verbalized her observation and asked why I come to sessions if I'm unwilling to talk about my feelings.

Huh?

Her question stopped me in my tracks.

She told me all I talk about is my kids and my difficulties managing work, the family, and the household—responsibilities many people undertake. My issue is I use unhealthy coping mechanisms to handle the physical symptoms that result from my constant worrying.

Last week in my support group, we spoke about how we can talk about the weather with our therapists or get to the meat and potatoes. (Sorry if the food reference disturbs you. It's not intentional.)

The topic coincided with the conversation I had with my therapist. She argued that if I wasn't willing to discuss my feelings and get to their root, we could work on acceptance instead because everything would remain business as usual.

A bit harsh, right?

I am blessed to have abundance in my life. It is the glasses I wear that could use an adjustment. They are scratched and smudged.

In response to what I considered an attack, I journaled and brought my entries to share with her. The result: we spoke about my feelings during the entire session. I didn't deviate or redirect, even though it wasn't a barrel of laughs.

She gave me the assignment to look at my various roles. Being a mother had become my identity. What else was there?

The second assignment was to use feeling words instead of "anxious" since anxiety is a state rather than a feeling.

Your Turn

Trauma is self-explanatory. There's no reason to relive it or elaborate when answering the first two questions.

Do you find you avoid specific topics to explore during therapy sessions?

Do you redirect a conversation when it hits a nerve?

Which feelings do you stuff and shy away from discussing?

Do you use blanket statements to describe them?

As I said, mine is "anxious." What is/are yours?

If you were to dig deeper, can you name the feelings buried underneath the blanket statements?

These are what we have to deal with.

You might want to discuss your responses with a professional. Who knows what you might discover?

Let's get digging because residing beneath the surface is where the truth lies.

In A Fix

My Turn

When I was a little girl, I loved watching the cartoon *Felix the Cat*. Whenever things got tough, Felix would reach into his bag of tricks.

I still have my Felix the Cat stuffed animal who has provided comfort through various life experiences.

When I showed my husband my drawing, he replied, "I don't get it." So, of course, I sang him the theme song. He didn't understand its relevance to ED.

To me, it's simple. We all have our "bag of tricks," which arms us with tools to make the right choice when we're struggling with ED. The longer we're in recovery, the more tricks we have to choose from to yank us out of our "fix" or difficulty.

With that said, I may have an array of tools, but the problem that arises is I forget—scratch that—*choose* not to use them and instead succumb to the peer pressure ED inflicts on me.

We went out with a few couples to a bar/restaurant. A girl sang in a band, and customers drank and enjoyed themselves—some more than others. My husband and I talked and laughed with our friends.

The conversations between the women at our table were typical. One spoke about the diet she was currently on, the other talked about a friend's body type, and then there were the discussions about working out.

These girlfriends have no idea about my relationship with ED because I'm overly selective with who I divulge that information.

The topics didn't faze me since I hear these types of comments often from women. What did faze me was ED scrutinizing other women in the bar as if each were in the bikini portion of a beauty pageant and how I compared in relation.

My husband was joking with the guys, talking about video games, sports, and work. And there I was, checking out women.

At the end of the evening, during our drive home, he asked if I had fun, and my authentic self uttered, "Not really." I didn't get into specifics about ED pretending to be a pageant judge because my husband was in good spirits, and I didn't want to bring him down.

It was nice to get out and socialize, but I realized going to a bar and seeing scantily-clad women provoked me and should be postponed until I'm more stable in my recovery.

My nutritionist told me that if I want to combat ED, I must remain angry at it and the power it holds over me. Becoming stagnant is dangerous. ED waits for weak moments to strike against me when I least expect it.

How do I remain angry at ED?

I write about my feelings, draw pictures, have date nights that incidentally trigger it, speak with my team, and go to a support group where its dangers get reiterated.

Fortunately, the tools in my bag are mine to keep. They are my survival kit to remind me of ED's presence and how I must fight against it round-the-clock.

Your Turn

How can you remain angry about ED's presence in your life?

What destruction has ED caused?

What are the consequences of giving into ED?

What can you do to keep the fire of hope inside you burning to fight against ED?

We can't sit back and pray ED will get bored and disappear. During moments of idleness, ED becomes more pronounced.

Have you noticed certain people, places, and things ignite ED?

How do you react?

Do you ignore ED?

Can you use your voice and not put yourself in vulnerable or provoking situations until you're ready?

If not, how can you prepare in advance for emotionally charging experiences to set yourself up for success?

Can you share your fears with a trustworthy source or bring a safe person with you?

I've been in situations where I've plucked my phone out of my purse and read jokes or inspirational quotes on Pinterest to interrupt ED's badgering.

We must stay angry at ED.

BINGO

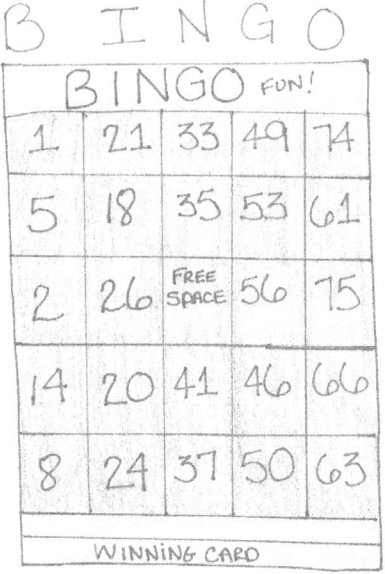

My Turn

Once again, I feel isolated from friends. I never allow myself to get too close to women.

I found a friendly group—mothers at the elementary school where my youngest attends.

Interestingly, I see myself in a different place maturity-wise. I'm older and have older kids. The women are also preoccupied with their bodies, food, and workout gear. I listen to their nonsense and let it flow in one ear and out the other without getting caught up in it. It doesn't trigger me anymore.

Why am I friends with these women with whom I have nothing in common?

I can use the excuse that my youngest is friendly with their sons, and we get together as groups, but the truth is loneliness plays a significant role.

****

Six years later, I'm adding to this entry.

When I look back, it's easy to see why I never let those women get close to me. There was too much gossip and superficiality in the conversations—a red flag for me to remain emotionally distant.

Engaging in gossip isn't my thing. It serves no purpose. Just as I keep my secrets locked inside, others do as well. We all have something to hide, which takes away my judging rights. Besides, I have enough going on in my life. Ruminating on other people's drama is a waste of mental space.

What I came to realize was those women had nothing worthwhile to offer me spiritually. It's not a judgment but a difference of personal interest.

I wanted to be part of a social group so desperately, I was willing to sell myself short and got hurt in the process. On many occasions, those women left me out. It was mean.

Unfortunately, it reinforced my isolation, especially from women, since they seem to burn me repeatedly. Beneath the hurt was rejection. Why didn't they include me?

I can't feed into those types of thoughts. They get me nowhere. Instead, I choose not to be around insensitive people, especially ones who disrespect me. I deserve the same respect I show others.

A close girlfriend was part of that original group. She was different. There was something about her that drew me to her. We both took a risk and opened up. The rest is history, and I'm blessed to have her in my life.

When someone upsets me, I have learned to share my pain without blame. Doing so cuts out the chance of misinterpreting the intent of another.

Your Turn

Who makes up your social circle?

Do these people have your best interest at heart?

Do you place yourself around people who test your recovery out of a need for acceptance?

I took a considerable risk hanging around those women. Their conversations didn't tempt me per se, but that's not to say the constant body talk and comparisons didn't get to me. Today, I know I'm more than my body. I prefer to be around others who share that view.

How do you feel when you're with people who trash-talk others?

Does insulting others to boost your esteem work to your benefit?

Do you find you open up to everyone and over trust?

If yes, what is the result of doing so?

Do you set boundaries by sharing certain information with specific individuals?

I share different levels of personal information, depending on my trust with the person.

When people around you focus on body talk and food, how does it affect ED?

Hint: ED loves body-shaming conversations.

If you find yourself in such a circumstance, what boundaries can be put in place to protect yourself?

Behind The Mask

My Turn

"You're so laid-back."

"You seem so calm."

These comments are frequently said to me, which I find hilarious.

I'm a master at hiding my feelings. I can be experiencing a full-blown panic attack, and other than my husband, who knows me to a T, nobody else would have a clue what's going on inside me. I hide it that well. Years of practice have made me a master.

Growing up as a child of an alcoholic, I learned my feelings didn't count. So, then why share them if nobody wants to hear them?

I carry a lot of shame. I already suffer from low self-esteem, so being judged by others doesn't boost the little self-confidence I have.

I've also learned that putting on a mask and wearing a happy face goes far. I can have a load of anxiety but still wear a smile.

Stripping off the make-up and going bare doesn't happen often, and when it does, it's only with a select few, as I've mentioned previously.

Thankfully, I have the utmost trust in my team. They get to see the real me that most people don't.

Who knows, maybe at some point, the mask will come off permanently, and I'll be brave enough to stand tall without a costume. Until then, the mask remains.

Your Turn

Do you show different sides of yourself to others?

Who do you show the real you to?

Do you wear a mask in public?

If so, do you ever feel safe enough to remove it? When?

Is it easy for you to share your feelings?

If not, what do you do with them?

How do you express them?

Are you able to sit with the "bad" ones?

I use quotation marks because feelings are neither good nor bad. It's how we perceive, cope, and react to them that gives them a good or bad label.

What would it take for you to be able to do so?

*****

Add-on during editing.

Can you visualize yourself feeling your feelings to the fullest without judgment?

Would you judge a friend who is baring their soul to you?

Imagine yourself bringing the same compassion you would give to that friend to yourself.

It's not easy, but it's something worth trying and striving for.

The Show Must Go On

My Turn

The Queen song "The Show Must Go On" is a metaphor for my life. Inside, my heart aches. I don't feel good enough, strong enough, or lovable enough. Regardless, my smile remains. It has to.

To me, the lyrics "The show must go on" represent shame and loss. I've watched the movie *Bohemian Rhapsody* three times in the past month. The first and second viewings were on plane rides to and from Europe, making the hours pass more quickly. The third viewing was at home. For whatever reason, the movie brings my emotions to the surface.

I know the film's ending isn't happy, yet Freddie Mercury recorded the song "The Show Must Go On" in one take, while sick with AIDS.

As sick as he was, he put on a smile and did his thing.

As sick as I am with ED, I put on a smile and do my thing.

There is an overwhelming sense of loss as the years pass—the progression of life. My children are becoming adults and moving on with their lives. It's so hard to let go and see myself aging in the process. Still, with tears in my heart, the show must go on.

Your Turn

Are you able to get up and do your thing even on your worst days?

Are you able to let the show go on amidst internal pain, or does it seep out in other areas?

If you could choose a song that's a metaphor for your life, what would it be and why?

How effective are you at letting go?

These might be past regrets, arguments, or hurts done by you or to you. Again, if there is past trauma, letting go should be explored with a trained professional.

How does holding on serve you?

Does it serve you?

Does it encourage ED to numb the pain?

What would it take to let go of the pain that no longer serves you?

Section VI
F**k ED

Audrey And ED

My Turn

ED behaviors discussed. Read with caution.

This particular journal entry comes in the form of a poem. I hope that my frustration with my eating disorder comes across.

Ben refers to my husband, whose name I changed to protect his privacy. Audrey refers to my anxiety disorder, and ED is ED (Boo, ED!).

So, without further ado, I present my poem about Audrey and ED.

This morning I woke up with three people in my bed,

One whose name was Audrey, one whose name was Ben, and then finally, there was ED.

Ben wanted to relax and cuddle. ED and Audrey wanted me up and moving about,

ED told me to exercise. Audrey was ready to clean. They are both so damned repetitive; they make me want to shout!

How many days have they won over Ben and the kids and taken time away from us?

They order me around every day, and I never put up a fuss.

For they know best how to make me feel good; how to cope with all that goes on around me,

ED has a PhD, so it must be right when it tells me to look in the mirror and find fault with what I see.

It tells me I can only be desirable because of how I look,

After all, that's what important. ED knows me like a book.

It doesn't matter what I think, especially how I feel,

ED simply tells me to eat less and exercise more, and then my stressors will be no big deal.

It tells me if I'm bloated, then I'm fat, and who would want me?

On those days, it pushes me even harder to look at myself in the mirror and like who I see.

They both tell me that without them, I will not be able to cope,

They both tell me that without them, I will never have any hope.

Audrey and ED are best friends. They work together as a team,

They tell me peace and serenity can only be found in a dream.

These two best friends wreak havoc. They think it's fun to play with my mind,

They surely aren't real friends. They're harsh, judgmental, and unkind.

I want them both to go away and just let me be,

I want to know what it's like to live life and, of them, finally be free.

Each day is a struggle like a child lost in a maze,

I can't find my way out—seconds turn into minutes, minutes into hours, and hours into days.

There has to be an answer. I'm told it's inside of me,

But with ED and Audrey taking up so much space, I feel like a prisoner inside trying to get out but have no key.

This morning ED told me to exercise. I was crawling inside my skin,

It gave me many justifications for why I should give in.

I felt angry.

I felt rage.

Will both of you please get out of my head!

It was finally my turn to tell them both, "Get off your high horses. You don't know what's best for me! F**k you, Audrey and ED!"

Your Turn

Have you ever told ED to f**k off?

What was the result?

Does ED promise to help you handle life?

What kind of self-talk do you hear yourself saying when you look in the mirror? I know this may be a difficult question to answer.

Write down ED's critique. Lay it all out on paper. You can look in the mirror and jot things down as they come up.

Set the paper aside.

Collect yourself.

Take a deep breath.

Look over your list.

It can be mind-blowing to see on paper the offensive words ED uses to describe us. It convinces us these false claims equate to our worth.

ED IS WRONG!

We are worth so much more.

****

Add-on during editing.

I am one who prefers to end on a happy note.

Look in the mirror and write down one thing you like about yourself. I love my eyes. The color is pretty. Fortunately, both of my sons inherited the light eyes gene from me. My daughter complains that she didn't.

Keep the paper by the mirror and continue to add compliments and praise. Maybe your hair is cooperating—write it down. Perhaps your outfit suits you and you could be on the cover of a fashion magazine—add it to the list. Perchance your eyes light up when you smile—jot it down.

If we can turn the negatives into positives, the positives will eventually become habitual, just like ED's nasty voice has.

We weren't born with ED's voice. It's a detrimental coping mechanism we picked up along the way.

The stories ED tells us are fictional. They don't exist.

Let's create a new nonfiction story of our lives. One that's guaranteed to have a happy ending. We can make that assurance because we are the authors and write the script. We create how the scenarios will play out.

I would never write a romance novel without a happy ending for the characters. Our stories should follow that same principle.

Attitude change is challenging but not impossible to achieve.

The Evil Scale

My Turn

ED behaviors discussed. Read with caution.

My husband learned my weight from my nutritionist. She had asked me to remove the scale from my house and do blind weigh-ins at her office. My husband hid it, but I managed to find it by looking in closets, underneath the bed—anywhere I assumed he might place it. I behaved like an addict searching for drugs.

Afterward, I was in awe. I demanded my husband ditch the damn thing altogether. Throw it away. Give it to someone. I didn't care what he did with it. I just wanted it out.

The fact my husband found out "my number," and I didn't, infuriated me.

During my meeting with my nutritionist, she went on to tell me how pleased she was with my progress. She may as well have stabbed me. I didn't take her praise as a compliment. Her comment meant one thing and one thing only: I had gained weight!

Anger, sadness, and fear took over because I was somehow losing control.

"Am I overeating?"

"What am I doing wrong?"

These questions roared in my head, the very ones that got me into treatment to begin with. After all, isn't the primary goal of recovery to become healthy, even if that means I'm not comfortable in my skin while doing so?

My eating disorder became enraged by this news. I felt anxious and distraught, which led me to write the following poem. I shared it with my treatment group the next morning.

How Can A Number Define Who I Am?

Why, when I look in the mirror, do I just focus on the shell?

Why is it so hard to decipher whether it's me or my eating disorder talking—why is it so hard to tell?

How can I think the size of my clothes somehow reflects the real me?

How is it my view of my body is so different from what others see?

How is it I can be hungry yet feel too full to eat?

Why does every meal sometimes feel like a feast?

It's not about the food. At least that's what I'm told,

I'm trying to control everything around me. Things I can't possibly hold.

Why do I suppress my feelings, stuff them deep inside?

Feelings I don't want others to know. Feelings I try to hide.

But they just keep sneaking out in so many different ways,

No matter how hard I try, I can't keep the overwhelmingness of them at bay.

Now is my time to speak up and let my feelings flow,

Because all they've done inside me is continue to grow.

They don't go away, they repeat themselves, they tell me to escape,

By eating less, exercising more, and putting on my Super Woman cape.

So then why is it this weight thing weighs so heavily on my mind?

How can one pound more on the scale erase all the hard work I've done and cause my behavior to rewind?

The thoughts are like maggots picking at my brain,

They are like standing outside in a hurricane, getting pounded by hail and rain.

I know thoughts pass with time, and I have to ride them out,

But at times, it's like being front and center at a rock concert where my thoughts are the starring attraction, and all I hear is them, and their fans scream, rant, and shout.

I must breathe, write, draw, sing, or sit quietly until the choir has sung its last song,

I must not listen when they tell me to do things I know are wrong.

They tell me if I keep my feelings stuffed, they will be safe and contained,

All I end up feeling is exhausted, tired, and emotionally drained.

So, I pose this question again. How can a number define who I am?

It does not. It does not. It does not.

The answer has been there all along. The number is just the outside. It's the inside I forgot.

Your Turn

Do you let a number define who you are?

With all our daily responsibilities, how can a single number on a scale make or break our day?

Even worse, we give the number so much power and let it directly impact how we view ourselves.

I'm tired of this insanity. Join me in my crusade against ED, and just for the moment, don't allow a number to define you as a person.

Instead, find something you enjoy, something that makes you happy or excites you, something that will lift your spirits and ultimately boost your confidence. After all, these are the real defining moments in our lives.

We are so much more than our eating disorders. They do not define who we are. Nor should we allow them to. And please, I beg of you, get rid of the evil scale. It's a weapon ED uses against us. It's a failure either way.

What The Hell Happened?

My Turn

I stepped on a scale.

How could this one little act throw me into such a tailspin?

I didn't tell anybody, either, which only made it worse.

The guilt began to eat at me, and I knew I had to be honest with my husband and team, or else ED would once again become my puppeteer.

****

Add-on during editing.

Over the years, I've learned that determining the number on a scale is a no-win situation.

If the number is too high for ED's liking, it will create havoc.

If the number is too low, my healthy voice will advise me to step up my game and fight against ED.

The ED voice can be loud, or it can be a mere whisper.

I have become attuned to the varying levels and can decipher ED's voice from my own. It took a while to get to this point in my recovery. Patience is a virtue.

We all make mistakes, relapse, stumble, and fall. We are human. The crucial next step when this occurs is to stand up and start again.

I have waited until the sun rises the following day to give recovery another go and still do occasionally. The difference is I no longer beat myself up for doing so.

Would you yell at a friend who screwed up?

I would hope the answer is no. With that being the case, why is it okay for us to yell at and belittle ourselves?

It's not.

Your Turn

Have you made a mistake(s) during recovery and found it challenging to get back on track?

It's okay to admit it has happened. Like me, you're human.

What kinds of things do you tell yourself when you fall?

Jot some of them down on paper.

Consider them.

****

Add-on during editing.

Let's take this idea a step further.

If you were an outsider looking in and reading what you wrote, would you think the words or statements are logical and realistic, and more importantly, kind and compassionate?

Would you offer insensitive words as advice to a friend or family member who is struggling?

It can be surprising to see how abusive our thoughts are on paper. They are the thoughts of our eating disorders, which tell us we don't deserve to recover, that we can't recover even though others can, that we are different, and that our situation is worse than everyone else's.

As hard as it is to believe, we are more alike than not.

Now, make a list of appropriate alternatives to the nasty comments previously written.

It might seem robotic to tell ourselves nurturing words. We must retrain our minds. ED has been controlling us, even possessing us on many occasions and telling us we are worthless and don't count. The script requires a rewrite.

Remember that new nonfiction story of our lives with the happy ending I spoke about in the Audrey And ED entry? Let's continue writing it.

Read over the new, uplifting words and statements and see how they compare to the unsympathetic ones.

Quite a contrast, right?

Are the new ideas more suitable to offer a distressed friend or family member?

How do you feel after reading the alternatives?

Become aware of the two voices.

As I said, it isn't easy, but eventually, we become able to distinguish between the two and accept that the healthy voice leads to recovery, whereas ED's voice leads to ruin.

Don't we deserve the same love and compassion we show others?

The challenge for the day is to tell yourself these new encouraging words. They might sound fake, but they will become the norm with practice, just like ED's harsh words did.

Remind yourself that ED's voice feeds you lies.

Expect ED to fight against this practice. It will do so with a vengeance.

If we continue to reprogram our thoughts with positive self-talk long enough, who knows, these ideas might become ingrained. We might start to believe we deserve more than to live a life bullied by an internal and cruel force of nature named ED.

Unlock The Door

My Turn

ED behaviors discussed. Read with caution.

It's incredible how easy it is to engage in self-destructive behaviors and find relief while doing so. Afterward, not so much.

Isn't that what addiction is all about?

Exercise has always been my preferred method of expelling energy and releasing anxiety. Who in the health profession would argue that these aren't proactive reasons for incorporating fitness into our daily lives?

My nutritionist felt terrible when she told me I had to cut back on physical activity. Too much of a good thing can have detrimental effects. Being both a personal trainer and a dietitian, she knows first-hand the health benefits exercise can provide.

My mind doesn't allow me to see myself as an over-exerciser. But just as with alcoholism or any other addiction, it isn't how many drinks, substances—the list goes on—one has or takes; it's the thought process behind the compulsion.

I have a distorted view of exercise. I have used it as a means to suppress my feelings and bury them.

The irony is I figured exercise was the perfect outlet to lessen my anxiety. Similar to drugs and alcohol, eventually, I needed more of it to achieve the desired benefit, which in the end, I wasn't getting. The anxiety was as horrific afterward as it was before I started because I didn't use my voice to create change.

It seemed the more I stuffed my feelings, the stronger the urge to expel my frustration through exercise.

Before treatment, I had been seeing the same therapist for years. I admired her outlook on life. From what I could tell, she had it all together. The problem was she never addressed my concerns about weight loss and over-exercise. Instead, she gave me homework assignments to better deal with stress.

I agree that taking time for myself is vital for my well-being, but I was drowning in my eating disorder. The obsessions and compulsions were all-consuming, and her "happiness" assignments did nothing. She wasn't an asset—try, a liability—because she didn't understand the beast that is an eating disorder.

Once I entered treatment, it became clear why it's imperative to find professionals who understand eating disorders. That therapist enabled me to continue along a path of self-ruin. In her mind, she was providing me with a beneficial service. Little did she know she was feeding into ED's ploy to destroy me.

Trusting the new psychiatrist assigned to me in treatment didn't happen overnight. It did develop, though, which is why he remains my physician years later.

****

Add-on during editing.

I have switched therapists several times since treatment, as some have pushed me harder than others. If given a choice, I would prefer to remain silent during sessions unless we're chatting about nonsense. My current therapist is firm with a gentle heart. In the words of Goldilocks, she is just right.

Prior to treatment, I felt suffocated by ED and helpless to recover. I can't stress enough the importance of a team, which usually consists of a therapist, dietitian, and psychiatrist, all of whom understand eating disorders.

I have also changed nutritionists. Some were too hard, meaning their expectations were too high, and some were too soft, meaning I could manipulate them when ED was controlling the wheel.

Similar to my therapist, my current dietitian is just right. She pushes me with caring hands, even when I screw up, which I do, a lot. But I continue to make progress. She praises small accomplishments, which remind me of my gains. Each one counts.

Your Turn

There can be instances where we get a sense that we are traveling alone on our recovery paths. Support is essential. Having a team that understands eating disorders is our oxygen. These people have the insight to help us find our voices and release feelings that are holding us captive, all while keeping a watchful eye on ED.

What I crave is to live a healthy and happy life. I must remind myself about this often, especially when ED tries to intervene and tell me otherwise.

How we respond to ED's voice is a choice, as harsh as this might sound. We are the only ones who can decide to move forward or stick with ED.

In my experience, whenever I let ED handle my stress, I end up worse for the wear.

How will you tell your unhealthy voice to take a hike?

We need to stand up to ED.

One day at a time.

One minute at a time.

One second at a time.

That is how we fight back.

What is one right choice you can make?

Do you have a knowledgeable support team?

If you are having difficulty putting one together, please see the Help And Support Are Available section at the end of the workbook.

As my dietitian says, each accomplishment counts. Do not discredit effort.

Just Go To Sleep

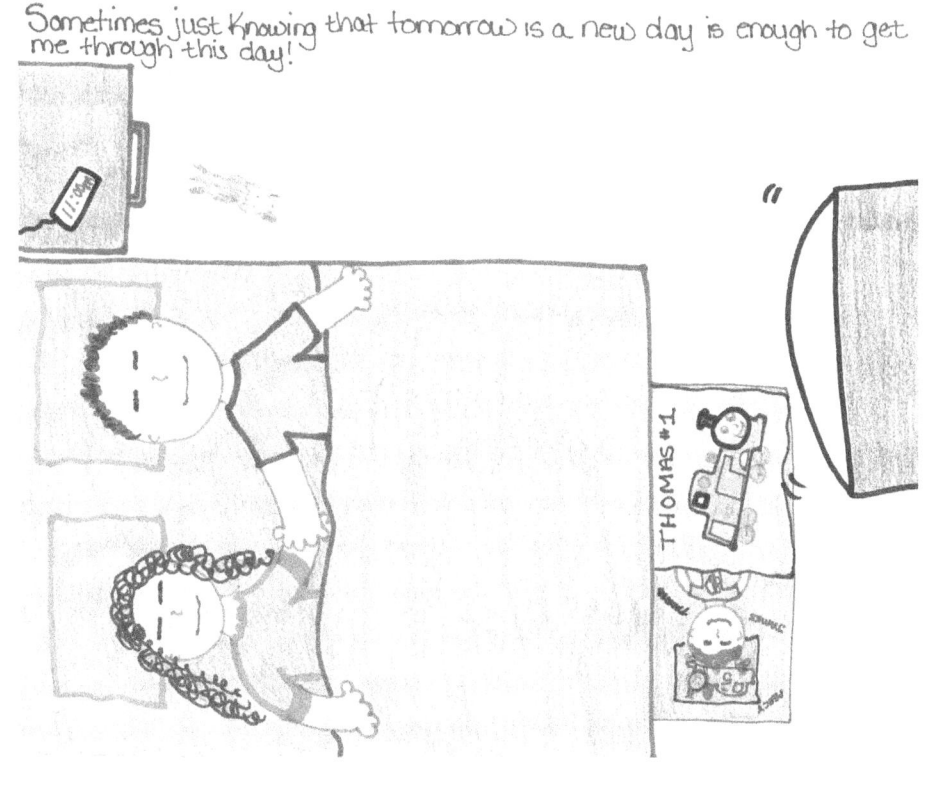

My Turn

On days when ED has confiscated my mind and body, I end up feeling rundown. I'll add guilt to the equation since I know I'm not making appropriate choices.

More often than not, the ED voice is so loud I have to pinch myself to stop myself from listening to it, leaving me to wonder where the hell my mind went.

When this happens, I find relief in knowing that tomorrow the sun will rise again. Sometimes that's enough to pull me through. I go to sleep with the awareness that when I wake up, I can restart my engine.

Recovery doesn't have to start at dawn, either. I can allow ED to have its way with me for as little or as long as I choose, or I can stop it in its tracks and resume recovery.

The sooner and faster I act, the stronger my pro-recovery voice becomes.

Your Turn

What can you do when ED badgers you, repeating commands and dictating orders left and right?

How can you muzzle that harsh voice?

If the image of a muzzle appeals to you, use it.

If your first choice or attempt doesn't work, have a Plan B ready. Be prepared to have a Plan C and D as well, just in case. We must always remain one step ahead of ED.

Don't limit the possibilities with your options. If something doesn't work, try something else.

These plans do not have to be set in stone. Remember, many paths lead to the same destination.

Now Playing

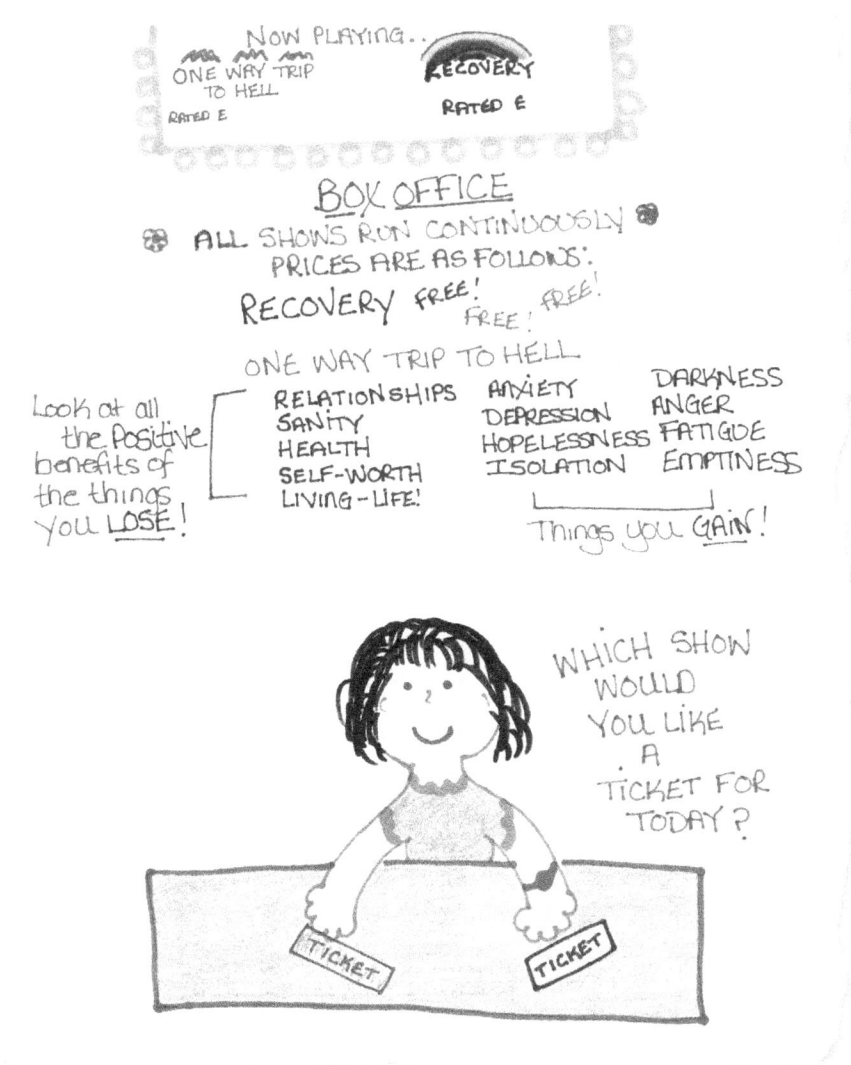

My Turn

Sitting in treatment and listening to patients read their "Who am I" packets was eye-opening.

A male patient told his story about a young life filled with abuse, divorce, drugs, jail, being kicked out of his home, etc. When he spoke about the concepts of love, women, and men and what they mean to him, his views were surprisingly optimistic.

A female patient shared her responses to the same packet. She, too, spoke of a troubled childhood. Her views were so pessimistic it was alarming.

Here were two people with similar life experiences but different outlooks.

I spoke with the female patient during a break. She commented that she would be in treatment forever. My reply was, "Why would you want to be?"

The incident got me thinking. A few days prior, I wasn't motivated and felt despondent regarding my recovery.

Listening to the female patient's bleakness about how her life was never going to get better was motivation enough to get me off my ass and back on the recovery path. Speaking to her was like looking in a mirror. I don't like seeing a forlorn version of myself.

I want the recovery ticket. I've been watching the *One Way To Hell Show* for too long, and it's way too scary for my taste.

Your Turn

What are the gains and losses you get by starring in the *One Way To Hell Show*?

How about the *Recovery Show*?

Every small step is a gain that CANNOT be taken away. Even two steps backward don't negate achievements.

The road to recovery never has traffic. It's always available, and you never lose the ground you've already covered.

Change... It's Time For One

My Turn

I have worn my hair long for many years. I feared cutting it, holding a false belief that I would look overweight.

This change in hairstyle has caused ED to blast me. It's been saying things like, "If you gain weight, you're going to look fat," and "Long hair is sexy and makes you look skinny."

ED has been badgering me nonstop.

I cut my hair as a way to say, "F**k you!" to that demonic ED voice. I also did it to take some of my power back.

Cutting my hair has nothing to do with my worth as a person. Neither does any physical change I make. My belief system and spiritual outlook do.

External changes might give me a temporary boost in confidence, but that quickly fades. Internal modifications and fighting against ED make the biggest and lasting impressions on my self-concept. It's quite a notion to embrace.

Your Turn

What false belief(s) have you been holding on to that keep ED in control of your behavior(s)?

It doesn't matter how odd they seem. Look at my example about my hair length determining my worth. ED loves to focus on idiocy.

What can you do to counteract these beliefs and kick ED out of the picture, even if only temporarily?

Go ahead, get that haircut, new hair color, or pair of shorts you've been excited about. But do it because you want to. Not because ED is forcing you to.

External motivators have their place but don't necessarily represent who we are at our core.

Hurdles

My Turn
(Behaviors discussed. Read with caution)

In the entry Filling Your Tank, I mention that I dropped an entire bottle of lotion on my baby toe, breaking it, in my mad dash to get everything done. What I didn't say was that we had a family vacation planned for the following week, and I couldn't put my foot in a shoe.

In addition to the toe incident, while engaging in compulsive exercising rituals, I hurt my back. I went to the orthopedist, who gave me a steroid shot and sent me to physical therapy.

My experience on our trip became that of an observer rather than a participant. During our trip, I went to the gym every morning and experimented with various exercises despite my injured back and toe.

What kind of self-preservation is this?

Would I allow my children to behave so irresponsibly if they were injured or hurt?

Would a person not suffering from ED treat their body with such disrespect?

How many messages do I need from the universe to stop this insanity?

I called my sister crying because breaking the cycle is so trying. She pointed out all the gains I've made. Pausing to let her words sink in, I realized she was right.

Daily hurdles set me back, but at least I push forward.

The biggest hurdle was my back injury. I have a bulging disc that I caused and had to go to a pain management specialist for another injection. The doctor informed me that I couldn't exercise for a week following the shot. I knew that wouldn't fly with ED, so I blabbed on it. I filled the doctor in on my eating disorder situation. He advised me to take it easy until my next visit and agreed walking would be acceptable.

I also went to the podiatrist, who gave me an open shoe and taped my toe.

When will enough be enough?

As a side note, my exercise addiction was in full swing prior to my third pregnancy. It had been for years. All exercise ceased when I learned about the pregnancy since the doctor considered me high risk being my first two children were preemies. My husband gave me weekly hormone injections to keep my uterus relaxed, which hurt like a bitch and made me depressed after each one. My focus throughout remained on the health of my baby. Nothing else mattered, especially not the size or shape of my body.

This example goes along with the question above. When will enough be enough? Why can't I show the same compassion to myself as I offer to my children?

Your Turn

Have you encountered any wake-up calls from ED?

Have they encouraged you to make healthier choices?

If not, what would it take to motivate you to fight against ED?

First and foremost, do you want to fight against ED?

Do you believe ED provides comfort and false security?

Is the clarity you're gaining in recovery bringing on more pain and suffering?

I have mentioned that awareness is our starting point. Then comes acceptance of having an eating disorder. Once there is recognition of a problem, we can proceed along the recovery path with others in the same boat. Remaining blindsided by ED keeps us stuck in its grips. The result isn't pretty.

Do You See What I See?

My Turn

I remember my art therapist in treatment, Sherry, asking me to do a life-size drawing of how I saw myself. She then taped the picture to a wall and had me stand against it. She traced an outline of my body using a different color.

Afterward, I studied how her outline differed from mine. How could my perception be so off?

I had a distorted body image. That was how.

Sherry was wrong. I told her I wasn't as thin as she drew me, even though she *traced* my body. I asked her to do another outline in a new color. She had to have made a mistake. She agreed, and her tracing yielded the same results as her first.

WTF?

Had ED taken such control over my perception that even with glasses, I didn't see clearly?

The answer was yes. ED tries to make me look in a mirror and see a body that isn't mine. But I knew what I saw. ED convinced me of that.

I got dressed the other night to see a show with my husband. I looked in the mirror, and judgments came flying. I could have been on *America's Next Top Model* for all the critiques I received from ED.

Taking a pause, I told my husband I was celebrating myself. He looked baffled. I repeated the words and finished dressing.

My husband and I went to dinner with my sister, brother-in-law, and niece. We had a blast. I could have let ED ruin my evening and make me change clothes, but I didn't. Not that ED would be satisfied with anything I put on, other than baggy pants and a loose-fitting top to hide my figure. The bonus: my teenage niece told me how cute my outfit was.

"See, ED, you aren't the fashion police—since you have no sense of style, doctor police—since you can't keep me healthy in a physical sense, or nutrition police—since you know nothing about healthy food choices and portion sizes. So stop chastising me, you ignorant jackass!"

****

Add-on during editing.

I saved the drawing from treatment. I wanted to see if, years later, I still had a distorted view of my body. I taped the paper to my bathroom wall with the original drawing face down, giving me a clean surface to work on. I used a colored marker and drew how I envisioned my body to look. I then stood next to my picture and had my husband trace me.

The outcome: my distortions had significantly lessened. I was almost spot-on. There was barely any difference between my perception of how I viewed myself and my husband's tracing of me.

Repeating this activity showed the growth in my recovery. I won't say I no longer have body image issues. They fluctuate in frequency. The difference is when I'm naked in the bathroom, I no longer stare in the mirror and dissect myself to pieces like I used to. I might even compliment myself.

When I become critical of my body, I practice gratitude for all it does for me. It enables me to live and breathe. It doesn't define me, even though ED argues against that factoid. ED wants a never-ending WWE Superstars match. I have learned to give it less airtime.

Your Turn

What type of cop is ED playing in your life?

What kinds of messages or judgments is it making against you?

What's your line of defense?

What can you do to prove ED wrong and show it how distorted its perceptions are?

Feel free to try the body-tracing activity. It's a helpful barometer to track changes in body perception.

May I Take Your Order?

My Turn

During one of my weekly groups, the facilitator spoke about how she was willing to give up certain ED behaviors when she first entered recovery but not others.

I am at that place again. Not that I ever left.

The battle between ED and my pro-recovery voice is ongoing. The one area where I continue to allow ED to control the reins is with my meal plan.

During our last session, my nutritionist told me she wanted me to add diversity to the foods I eat. She said once I do that, ED will be far off in the distance because I'll be fighting back.

Her words sounded optimistic and hopeful. Anyone in their right mind would say, "You've got this! Let's add diversity!"

The problem is, I'm not just anyone. I'm someone who lives with an eating disorder. I have a comfort zone that decides what foods I allow in my body.

Has it expanded? Definitely. I'll eat things now I wouldn't have in the near past, but that black cloud of fear still hovers over me. If I expand and allow myself to eat "forbidden fruits," then ED chimes in with all its opinions. I don't want to end up where I started. I've come too far.

Tonight at my support group, we spoke about taking baby steps in recovery. We have to move from A to B instead of A to Z. My over-achieving self wants to get through the entire alphabet in a day.

I've taken baby steps as far as my meal plan is concerned but am far from reaching Z. My path is a journey, not a destination or endpoint.

I'm hopeful the diversity my nutritionist suggested gets incorporated into steps B to C or even C to D. As long as I'm moving ahead, I'm moving in the right direction.

ED still reprimands me and is abrasive in its tone. I acknowledge its presence but don't give in to its demands as much as I used to.

I can endure a wide range of feelings and fully understand that when I allow ED to control me, they don't go away. Instead, they double in intensity. When ED wins, nobody wins. ED's desire for me is self-destruction into nonexistence.

Is that what I want?

Is that how I want to live the only life I am blessed to have?

The answer to both is a definite no.

Your Turn

Do you want to live a life of self-destruction into non-existence?

What baby steps can you take, even if only one, to put ED in its place and show it who's boss?

We are human with various likes, dislikes, and feelings.

What can you do today to add variety and not run from things you view as unfavorable?

Feelings come and go, like thoughts. They don't last forever.

A half-step forward is progress.

Remaining stagnant—*temporarily*—is progress.

Falling and getting up is progress.

How can you acknowledge ED's harsh voice and do the exact opposite of what it demands?

How Dare You!

My Turn

My support group discussed the notion of feeling somewhat insulted when someone tells us we look healthier or better after entering recovery.

Only in the mind of a person suffering from ED is that offensive. ED captures a golden opportunity with these compliments, telling us they are rude and offensive.

Warning: BEWARE and DISREGARD ED when you receive compliments.

As we begin to recover, our bodies go through physical changes. Outsiders will and do take notice. Some may even be vocal about it. There is no malicious intent meant by those who are on our side.

The question we must ask is, "Why did we choose to enter recovery?"

If the answer is, "To get healthy or better," then we are indeed on the right path.

ED doesn't want to hear praise because it means it's losing staying power over us. It goes against everything an eating disorder stands for, which is to keep us sick.

Your Turn

How do you react when someone gives you a compliment about your physical appearance?

What do you tell yourself in return?

If the words are critical, is ED talking or your pro-recovery voice?

Brainstorm and write compliments others might tell you regarding the physical changes taking place in your body.

Write down what ED's response to hearing such atrocities would be.

Next, write down what your recovery voice's response would be.

Compare the lists.

It is fascinating to see how different our authentic voice and ED's voice are.

The Endless Debate

My Turn

ED says one thing. My recovery voice says another. It's a continuous argument between ED's harassment and the part of me that wants to heal.

The internal back and forth is exhausting. The more I try to fight against ED, the louder the voice becomes to the extent I can't take it anymore and want to give in to silence it.

It's like listening to a lousy song on replay, over and over again. It never stops. It never shuts up.

My pro-recovery voice's rebuttals to ED's vile comments about physical appearance changes (How Dare You! entry) gave me further insight into how distorted and irrational it is. Not that I didn't already know. Reinforcement about its cruelty never hurts, though.

It isn't easy to contradict every toxic comment because they come lightning fast in speed rounds. I want to cover my ears to silence them but can't because they're inside my head. The hard part is mentally challenging ED's abusive slurs.

Your Turn

What do you do when the internal debate gets exhausting and you want to silence ED? Do you give in to it, or do you fight it?

Do you find it's getting easier to dispute it now that you have some tools in your bag of tricks?

What are some rebuttals you can write to ED's nasty comments?

Can you recognize ED's nasty comments?

If not, you will. Don't lose hope. *Never* lose hope.

Section VII
False Sense Of Control

To Eat Or Not To Eat

My Turn

There's a sense of relief over the recognition that my eating disorder has an enormous amount of control over me. It has me strapped to chains bound so tight I can't free myself from it.

I know once I truly surrender to the reality that I have a life-threatening illness that requires medical care and treatment, or else I'll lose my life to it, I'll find liberation from the disorder's hold over me.

Control affects all aspects of my life. It is this very power I falsely believe I have over everything and everyone around me that creates anxiety, which manifested itself into an eating disorder.

I try to govern everything from when the dogs bark to when the mail comes. I have somehow taken on this belief that I can do God's job. It seems so egotistical to see this admission in writing. But when we try to oversee the goings-on around us, aren't we, to a certain degree, trying to play God?

I don't want that job. It's taken, and I'm far from qualified for the position.

A fellow patient was sitting across from me in our treatment group, sharing about the obstacles she faces with her eating disorder. "To eat, or not to eat" instead of "To be, or not to be" came to mind.

These are related ideas when I consider them from a philosophical standpoint. If I choose to eat, I am choosing to be, which is to live life. If I choose not to eat, I am choosing not to be present, which is giving up the fight to exist.

My eating disorder wants me to remain sick. The light inside me wants me to be healthy.

I hadn't had glimpses of my inner light in forever until I entered treatment. I've started to sense its presence again.

The undertaking to remain balanced comes from juggling thoughts that try to persuade me to hold ED's hand versus my new awareness that I can select an alternate route.

Your Turn

In what ways are you still trying to control everything around you?

Do you presume to have power over others, situations, and events?

How is that working?

I can assume it isn't, even though I shouldn't make assumptions about what's going on in other people's minds.

How does this desire to manage things around you affect your behavior? Your feelings? Your thoughts?

What can you do to let go of one thing—big or small—which is out of your control?

I'm challenging you to take the opportunity because it is one. It might not feel as such, but it is.

What goes on internally after realizing the only influence you have over outside factors is your response and reaction to them?

Powerlessness equates to freedom in my book. We can let go of our longing to control the stuff we have no power over. It's not an easy idea to accept, but inner calm follows once we put it into practice.

We aren't God.

If you don't believe in a Higher Power, feel free to substitute something else that works better for you, i.e., controller of the universe, universal energy, Jesus Christ.

The job of God already has an excellent CEO. Sorry to say, there isn't a help-wanted sign. Our assistance isn't warranted.

Yeah! I Am Imperfect

My Turn

My morning meditation was about being imperfect. I loved it and mused about it all day. How wonderful it is not to have to do everything perfectly.

If only I could believe it.

It is here where the practice of acceptance comes into play. The world won't fall apart if a bed is left unmade, laundry remains in a basket, or dirty dishes hang out in the sink.

These are also the moments when I have to stop trying to do it all and ask for help. Doing so translates into all aspects of my life. I can't assume or expect others to volunteer their services. They are busy living their lives. I have to express my wishes.

Ugh! It's so darn hard to do that when I grew up believing my voice had no worth.

Your Turn

Do you ask for help?

Do you reach out when you need to talk?

What can you do when you are overwhelmed to relieve some of that pressure?

Tell yourself you are imperfect because you are. We all are. Look in the mirror with a smile and tell yourself it's okay to be the imperfect, perfect you.

High Jump Of Expectations

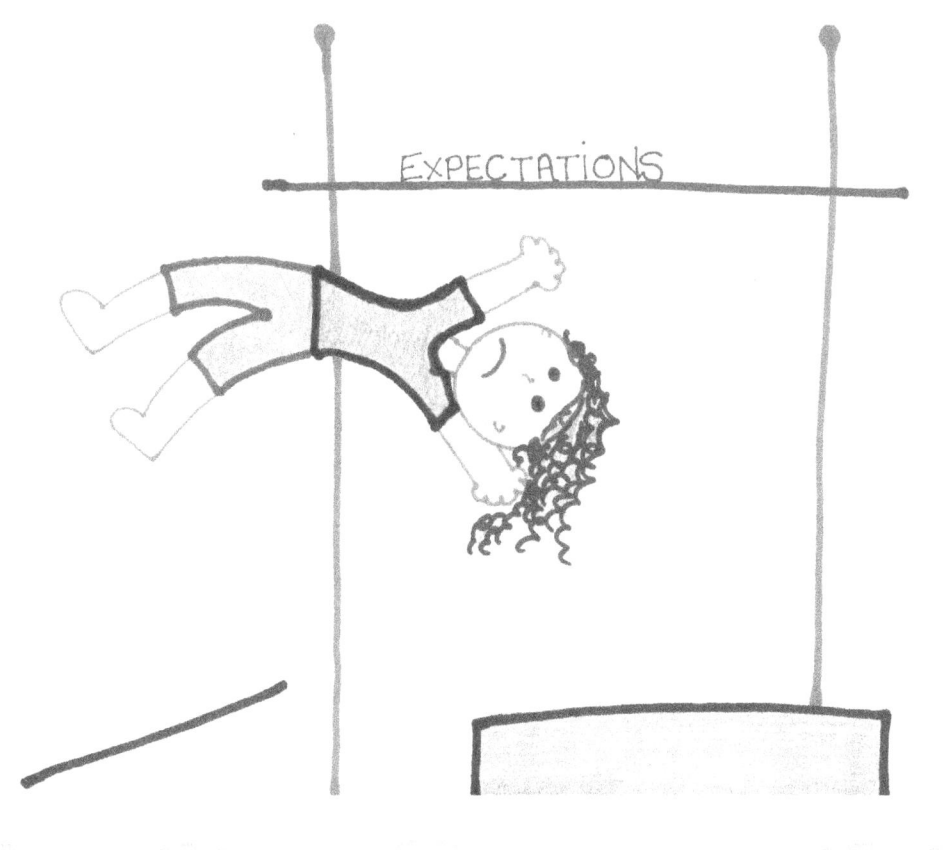

My Turn

Falling short of expectations.

Why is it I feel herculean? That I can do it all and then some, only to feel more anxious and incapable?

Everybody around me expects me to do things for them when, in reality, I'm the one putting high expectations on myself to perform without any assistance.

Until I learn to say no, I will never get relief. I am not superhuman.

There, I said it. This goes along with the To-Do List entry.

Trusting someone else's competence comes into play here since I believe my way is the best, and others are ill-equipped to do things to my standards.

The desire to control feeds into my over-achieving mentality. ED steps in and convinces me that since I can't control external events or others, I should control the one thing I can: what I feed my body and how much exertion I put on it. It tells me I *must* have control, or else everything will feel *out* of control.

Merely reading over this entry produces anxiety.

Control.

It's all ED wants when it can't have its way.

Your Turn

Do you ever feel superhuman and believe you can do it all?

Do you counteract these false beliefs?

Do you succumb to them?

If so, what can you let go of?

I have gained clarity from my assumptions about what I think others expect of me—also from nixing the idea that I know what's going on in another person's head. I'm not a mind-reader.

How about you? Do you make assumptions about how other people think and feel?

It has been my experience that doing so is a losing battle. And even if it wasn't, my head has no room for neighbors. It has enough stuff in it. Others can keep their own.

Yard Sale

My Turn

ED behaviors discussed. Read with caution.

We spoke at my support group about holding on to a piece of ED in recovery— surrendering some of it but wanting to keep a small part. It's a topic that comes up repeatedly.

I met with my nutritionist, who said my meal plan revealed ED-like eating. And here I thought I had been doing well. Sure, my snacks and meals weren't exactly what she prescribed, but I rationalized my behavior by saying I was eating more than I had before.

We discussed my exercise regimen. I informed her I had been adhering to her request that less is more, and as a result, the compulsions to over-exercise lessened. Yay!

When we reviewed my meal log, everything turned to crap. Seeing was proof I was eating "safe" foods and not venturing out of my comfort zone.

The acknowledgment I'm still dancing with ED and am willing to try some suggestions, but not others, is disappointing.

Trying new meals and snacks shouldn't be a difficult concept to grasp. For me, it's out of my depth. It shows ED's influence over me.

Every day is a push and pull of tug of war. Sometimes I'm oblivious about playing the game. I call it denial awareness.

To recover, I must fully surrender. I'm not there yet.

Your Turn

Are you holding on to a part of your eating disorder?

If yes, in what ways?

Do you recognize you might be holding on to some part of it?

How does this serve you?

Does it serve you?

****

Add-on during editing.

Holding on to a part of ED doesn't serve me. That said, bits and pieces remain on a leash. Years later, this has been the hardest brawl to win against ED.

Power Struggle

My Turn

Every day is a power struggle to do the next right thing. Some easier than others, but that's not to say there isn't one, especially when my hormones are going haywire.

I want my power back from ED. The security of living with what I know prevents me from taking a risk.

To an outsider reading this, it sounds messed up. It is. ED creates a mess in our minds.

ED tells me it helps me cope.

Does it?

Sure. If I consider self-harm beneficial to my well-being.

The power struggle is right versus wrong. It involves listening to my recovery voice rather than ED's trash talk.

My nutritionist tells me I should be mentally exhausted every day. She says I have to listen for ED's voice because it will sneak in and try to confuse my rational voice of reason.

Taking my power back means fighting against ED every second with no commercial interruptions.

Your Turn

What is your power struggle like with ED?

How does ED rear its ugly face?

Does it try to make you believe you're doing the right thing when, in fact, you aren't?

ED is a master manipulator.

Write some ways you can take your power back.

For an experiment, jot down one of the ideas you wrote on a sticky note and keep it within reach for a twenty-four-hour period. Use it as a reminder to fight that evil voice criticizing you.

Where In The World Is Matt Lauer?

My Turn

Before being called out for making sexual advances on co-workers, Matt Lauer did an annual segment on the *Today* show called "Where In The World Is Matt Lauer?"

Most people are too preoccupied with themselves to care about what others are doing.

While I was drawing, I went to erase a pencil mark, and the page ripped. I took a deep breath and told myself, "It's okay. It doesn't have to be perfect." I grabbed some tape and slapped it on the picture to repair it. Having such a calm reaction to something I put so much effort into isn't the norm for me.

I'm traveling overseas with my immediate family and my husband's family. It will be the farthest I have ever traveled. Thoughts of food and exercise consume me. So much will be out of my hands.

I'm trying to focus on the pros: seeing someplace new, getting together with my sister who lives in the country we're visiting, and sharing an exciting adventure with my husband and children.

The trip is frightening for me, though. I'll be leaving the safety of home, and my entire routine will get disrupted by schedules, time changes, and extended family interactions. This last one is a biggie. Spending prolonged periods with my husband's family can be taxing.

I have two choices. I can go into the experience preoccupied with all the "changes" I'll have to deal with, or I can view it as a once-in-a-lifetime opportunity that I may never get again.

I'm going with option two. ED is telling me I'm making a mistake. We're duking it out. The result is me refusing to miss out on creating memories with my children by letting ED win this battle.

Your Turn

How do you handle change in your routine?

Does the ED voice get stronger during these times?

Has ED caused you to miss out on opportunities because you've become preoccupied with it?

What would it look like for you to handle these scenarios differently and get to engage in them?

****

Add-on during editing.

Picture yourself succeeding at a challenging task or opportunity.

How can you rephrase your inner dialogue to words of encouragement rather than fear and doubt?

Write down pessimistic thoughts that arise when you think about change.

Take a break.

Reread what you wrote with an open mind and clear eyes, not ED's.

Do the words seem logical?

Can you see ED's manipulation and how its voice argues against anything that separates you from it?

Wouldn't it be great to say, "Where in the world is ED?" Then answer, "Who cares?" and hope it jumped ship, never to be seen or heard from again?

Self-Preservation

My Turn

I'm pondering the question my therapist posed. What makes me happy?

Little things like my kids' achievements, cuddles, my husband's words of love, music, and creative writing are a few.

In this instance, I'm referring to inner happiness in a spiritual sense. Isn't that the purpose of soul-searching, to dig through the dirt to uncover my true self?

Tonight at my support group, we spoke about acknowledging and denying ED. One member stated she doesn't see the consequences of it in her life. When she's alone, she isn't hurting anybody by engaging with it and hasn't suffered any physical effects.

A debate took place and sparked a discussion about it. The main rebuttal was about the physical consequences that can occur as a result of ED. When they haven't transpired personally, it's easy to see how ED hasn't caused any. YET. Give it time.

Emotional consequences were next.

Click! Many lightbulbs turned on in the group.

I face denial regularly. ED tells me that since I've achieved a healthy weight, it's okay to stick to my regimented and restrictive meal plan—emphasis on the word "my."

My nutritionist's meal plan for me is entirely different from the one I follow.

The denial is a coping mechanism to continue to engage with ED to deal with life instead of doing that soul-searching I spoke about above.

So, what are the negative consequences of my eating disorder?

There are too many to mention. Here are a few:

1. Isolation - to protect me from my shame about ED.
2. Isolation - to protect me from being accountable. If I tell others my ED behaviors, they might call me out when they see them. Why would I want that?
3. Isolation - to protect me from rejection. If others learn my truth, they might not like me. It's easier to wear a happy face and tell them everything is fine and dandy.
4. Isolation - to protect me from life. Being alone feels safe.

Realistically speaking, being alone, remaining inside my head, and shutting others out, gets lonely.

I'm tired of feeling lonely.

The therapist was right in her observation that I keep myself busy to avoid feeling. When I'm alone with my thoughts, they can be daunting. It's easier to busy myself with tasks. The problem is it gets physically and mentally tiring. Running on the mouse wheel nonstop is exhausting.

After therapy, I walked to the beach since it is near the office. I sat on a towel and took a half-hour just to be. I painted my nails, inhaled sea air, watched kids play in the ocean, and listened to tourists talk about their travel plans. I immersed myself in the moment and felt a glimpse of living rather than surviving.

A week ago, my nutritionist suggested I enter partial treatment again. I declined. That wasn't what I saw as the answer. Switching to a different therapist was. It was the kick start necessary to bring me back to a place of hope in recovery. The new therapist offers a fresh perspective, and once again, I'm back on track.

It's been almost a year since I entered recovery.

Has it been easy? No.

Fun? No.

Worthwhile? Yes.

I'm evolving, continually learning something new about myself. I scoop out another pile of dirt and see shimmers of light shining from within, only for the hole to get buried again.

I'm in no rush. I'm on a mission to figure out what makes me happy from within and gain inner strength and confidence. The only way I've found to accomplish that so far, as I've stated, is to feed my spirituality.

Your Turn

What makes you happy? It's an easy enough question to answer.

I'm kidding. It's not.

Reflect on the question and write about what comes up for you.

Have you suffered any physical consequences of ED?

How about emotional consequences?

How do you feel about this?

If anger and frustration arise, write about it. ED is frustrating. Scribble on paper to release the anger. Hit or scream into a pillow. Don't stuff it, but more importantly, be kind to yourself.

We didn't ask for ED, but we can learn to manage without its stupid advice.

Blah! Blah!

My Turn

ED behaviors discussed. Read with caution.

This entry is a continuation of the Self-Preservation entry.

At my weekly group, a woman spoke about not seeing the consequences of ED. At first, it fueled denial but left me considering it all week. So much so, I brought the topic up to my therapist and nutritionist.

The group spoke about looking at the physical aspects of what can happen when we engage with ED. Again, we talked about the emotional elements afterward.

It goes back to the irrational belief that I can hold on to a part of ED. If I change A and B but hold on to C, it's okay because my weight is stable. I mean, wasn't the purpose of treatment to get me back to a safe physical state?

ED tells me it was. It's wrong.

My nutritionist told me my rationalizations keep me in ED's grip, a grip that will get tighter the longer I listen to its lies.

Understanding this, does it take away the validity of what the woman said about not being physically affected by ED?

No.

I've been told awareness without behavior change will not lead to recovery. Okay. I get it, but I remain hesitant about the behavior change component, which means I'll adjust A and B, but not C.

To challenge myself, I agreed to text my nutritionist pictures of my meals until our next appointment for accountability purposes. It's infuriating to have to do this, but it's obvious I'm having grave difficulty being accountable to myself when it comes to ED. I keep letting it win regarding my meal plan.

The thoughts of what can happen and might happen if I don't modify my behaviors get brushed aside.

By agreeing to do this homework, I'm taking a small step to do something different.

Last night I didn't text her because I did what I wanted meal wise.

Today, I'll come clean because, in the end, I'm only harming myself by protecting ED.

ED thrives on secrecy. Its ultimate goal is to take over my mind, similar to how a cult brainwashes innocent victims.

ED is brainwashing me.

The only escape is to reach out to knowledgeable people who have my best interest at heart. I obviously don't because if I did, I wouldn't be treating my body that does everything for me in such an abusive manner.

So much guilt resides because of this insight. Once again, I'm practicing meditation, trying to remain present, and reading affirmations.

Just for today, I will live in the moment, even if I have to endure anxiety and fear in it.

Just for today, I will abide by the principle that awareness is only the first part of the equation in recovery; behavior change must follow.

Just for today, imperfection is acceptable. Like last night with my meal plan, I won't ace every test.

Just for today, I will learn from my mistakes and move forward.

Just for today, I will do something different and healthier, regardless of how small.

Your Turn

Just for today, what small step toward recovery can you take?

Texting my nutritionist stinks. I dread it because I know someone else is seeing my dance with ED.

What are some false rationalizations ED tells you?

How can your pro-recovery voice challenge them?

Do you accept the physical and emotional dangers of ED?

Do you see any physical and emotional dangers of ED *yet*?

If the answer is no, at some point, it will become a yes to both.

What would it take for you to open your eyes to see the severity of the illness in all regards—mentally, spiritually, emotionally, and physically?

How can you be accountable to do the right thing when it comes to ED?

Sleeping Beauty

My Turn

How do you hurt so deeply for someone you barely knew?

Feel pain in your heart and the rest of you too?

A few hours spent revealing deep-rooted fears,

Speaking about a sickness that possessed her for so many years.

The hurt I feel not only comes from the loss,

But also the realization that ED was her boss.

It took her where it wanted to, to her bitter young end,

No chance now to free herself from whom she thought was her friend.

ED tells us it'll help us, help us deal with our fears,

What we don't know is, we're just stuffing our tears.

I feel such pain for the young girl I barely knew well,

Because I know the torment she felt, living with ED means living in hell.

My tears, they are falling, like hail in a storm,

For losing someone I know to ED, my heart feels broken and torn.

I always hear stories about how deadly ED can be,

ED denies this truth and says it won't happen to me.

Now it's close to home, it's real, and I'm scared,

I don't want to be another victim of its cruelty, another innocent life spared.

I'm angry. I'm sad. I still see her beautiful face,

Sleep well, Sleeping Beauty. You're at peace now. You're safe.

Losing someone from my support group has been both mortifying and heartbreaking. The reality that ED ultimately leads to death if we don't stop the insanity heightens my fears.

We always hear about how eating disorders are the deadliest of all addictions because we need food to survive. Logically this is easy to comprehend, and yet, I continue to engage in the life and death battle.

Here she was, a beautiful college-aged girl who looked happy and content. Her past consisted of multiple treatment rounds. She came to the group at the suggestion of the out-patient ED program she attended.

Years of abusing her body ultimately led to her death. A life lost too young. It's not right!

This experience threw me for a loop. After processing it with my therapist, she expressed her concern that even after what happened to that sweet girl, I still had my stubborn shoes bolted to the ground, refusing to lift them. My therapist was insensitive and aggressive. No therapist had ever spoken to me in such a forthright manner.

Anger filled me. Luckily, she couldn't hear my inner screams aimed at her. They weren't pleasant.

She was right, though.

I felt like she had beaten me up. After our session, I cried for hours. I knew if she sat by and enabled me to continue with ED behaviors, it wouldn't serve me in the long run.

Intellectually I knew what I had to do. Logically I knew what the right thing to do was. Physically my body was tired. Spiritually I was and remain hopeful.

As content as I am living—surviving—with ED and an anxiety disorder, my hope doesn't diminish. If I weren't optimistic about something better, I wouldn't be writing these words.

Two steps backward. One step forward. The dance steps of ED. Each step backward does NOT mean I'm back where I started.

The beauty of recovery is it can begin morning or night. It doesn't matter when as long as the decision is made.

This reminder of how deadly ED is must remain at the forefront of our minds. It's not a game. It's not a joke.

I can now say I know someone who lost her life to ED. My wish is that her loss is my gain in winning my war against it.

I hope my message is enough for you, too, so that you don't have to lose someone you know either, or worse, lose your life to this hideous disorder, as well as open your eyes to the severity of it.

Your Turn

What can you tell yourself as a reminder that ED is only out to kill you?

These are strong words, but they speak the truth. This entry proves it.

How can you remove one bolt from your shoes so that you can take one baby step forward?

****

Add-on during editing.

My Turn Again

This experience proved how short life is. Even on my worst days, I have so much to be grateful for. It comes down to my attitude and perspective.

Today I am grateful for:

The health of my family.

My intuition and inner guidance.

How far I have come in recovery.

My ability to write romance novels along with being a published author.

Having a roof over my head and food on the table.

My team, my children, my husband, my dogs, my mother, my family, my friends, and my Codependency Anonymous group.

Open-mindedness to write this book and put myself out there after years of delay.

Freedom to explore my interests.

The ability to eat a meal and be okay with it.

No longer having to exercise to the point of pain.

Listening to my body.

The wisdom I gained from my dad.

The love I receive from my family.

The list continues.

Your Turn Again

No matter the circumstance, there is always something to be grateful for. ED disagrees and only wants us to see darkness.

What are you grateful for, and why?

It's easy to get caught up in what we wish for and if only. How about appreciating what we have right now?

Make a gratitude list. Gratitude comes in varying sizes, as we do. We can be grateful for the most minuscule of things. They count as much as the grand gestures.

Section VIII
Build A Toolbox

Helpful Tools In My Recovery

My Turn

When I first entered treatment, I kept hearing about ED. I thought people were referring to a patient. I finally asked about this ED character and was told ED stood for "eating disorder" and that I would learn about it soon enough.

The group therapist advised me to read *Life Without Ed* by Jenni Schaefer and Don Miguel Ruiz's *Four Agreements*. Both books were great reads, filled with valuable information and suggestions for change.

Other things I found helpful included:

A meal plan—one tailored specifically for me and something I wasn't keen on. I still don't jump up and down over my nutritionist's recommendations. I do give them a try, though.

Daily meditation.

Journaling.

Limited forms of gentle physical activity.

Pleasure reading—trashy romance novels are my favorite.

Listening to music.

Sharing what's going on. This component came easy during treatment because of the safety factor.

Art Therapy. One of the greatest gifts I received in treatment. It turned into this book.

Creative writing.

Your Turn

What tools have you found to be valuable in your recovery?

If you haven't found any, I'm willing to share mine.

What positive thing(s) are you doing for yourself?

Try to come up with at least one.

****

Add-on during editing.

Feeding yourself nourishing food counts, as does seeing your therapist and nutritionist. Taking a deep breath and pausing when ED is yelling at you is also a win. Let me not leave out reading a magazine, playing a game, and taking a bubble bath.

The little things we do for ourselves that bring us joy all qualify as self-care. Please don't let ED sneak in and tell you it brings you joy. It's lying.

How does it feel to acknowledge you are already doing beautiful things for yourself?

Don't take any positives for granted. The items you blow off as dumb or useless might just be the most beneficial tools in your recovery box.

It's not always easy to think of things that bring us happiness when we're in a funk. I've had to force myself to take a break. Being anal-retentive makes it that much more challenging.

All I'm suggesting is that you try doing something kind for yourself. If you aren't in the right frame of mind to do it for yourself, do it for someone else. You will still gain the benefit of the action.

****

Additional add-on during editing.

I recently heard a suggestion that might be helpful when we feel we don't deserve "me" time.

Write a permission slip on a sticky note to do something we enjoy. Start with one and progress to more.

10 Minutes… 10 Minutes

My Turn

ED behaviors discussed. Read with caution.

During treatment, my nutritionist suggested I limit exercise to three days a week. What the f**k? The result was waking up daily with strong compulsions. I was climbing the walls and didn't know what to do with myself.

I remembered a strategy given to me during one of the groups. It was to do three things—same or different—in ten-minute increments to combat or ride out a compulsion until it subsides.

I tried it out.

First, I drew for ten minutes.

Next, I played on my computer.

Whew. I had done it.

Yes, I was supposed to do three intervals, but fortunately, the compulsion passed in two. It didn't go away completely, but the activities distracted me enough not to act out on the compulsion.

There were no fireworks with a big crowd shouting, "Hurray!" and my anxiety remained high, but I worked through it and didn't give in to ED.

****

Add-on during editing.

In case you were wondering, the three-day exercise limit wasn't a success. It was an unrealistic bar to reach. It's an area I still address. Fortunately, there has been improvement.

My current dietitian and I agreed I could perform various types of activities for shorter intervals. My level of movement has significantly decreased, as has the kind I engage in. I am less focused on burning calories via cardio and more attuned to how my body feels during gentler workouts, i.e., barre.

When the obsessions and compulsions are intense, it's hard to walk away from them. Quite often, it's easier to give in to quiet the mind.

My over-exercise caused injuries. I am *choosing* milder forms of movement to prevent further damage. In the past, nothing would have stopped me. It was never enough. Today I have tremendous respect for what my body can and can't do—another success.

****

My therapist encouraged me to view life as a pizza. If the food reference disturbs you, try visualizing a clock instead.

The diagram of my life is divided into slices. A considerable portion gets allocated to my family. Other pieces are assigned to recovery, work, and marriage, to name a few. They are not proportional.

My mission is to balance the slices so that I allot a more substantial part to myself. Things like spirituality, creative writing, and other simple pleasures need to be incorporated more often to handle the other slices better.

Of course, shit happens, which means slices will vary in size depending on the circumstances. The piece that must remain consistent is my own. The minute I take away from it, the higher my anxiety level and louder my ED voice will get. Overwhelmingness will set in, along with the false belief that I can't handle what life is throwing at me. This reference has been so impactful I used it in one of my romance novels.

Your Turn

Look at your pizza or clock. Draw a circle with slices of varying sizes to represent various areas of your life.

Did you include a piece devoted to self-care?

What aspects are missing that need attention?

What can you do to balance the slices?

Keep in mind sizes will vary depending on life circumstances.

Which slices could use more space?

Now, envision how you would like your pizza or clock to look. You can draw another circle for this new representation.

Write what you would like to have inside the slices.

The key to this activity is to be realistic and set achievable goals that move you forward in recovery.

Unfortunately, it has been my experience that my slice always needs the most attention.

****

Add-on during editing.

It has taken years for me to give myself a hefty slice. Initially, my portion was minuscule. There have been instances where I've had to force myself to give myself the attention I deserve. When I slack on self-care, my mood turns crappy, and old patterns creep back in.

Do The Next Right Thing

My Turn

After cutting my hair, I had a two-day breather where ED rested. Maybe ED was ready to take a permanent vacation. The voice was getting softer. It was so refreshing.

And then, BOOM! It came back with a vengeance. It must have heard my satisfaction.

My armor was to keep repeating, "Do the next right thing," as the facilitator from my support group always says. It has become my mantra for the week.

When I'm not hungry, I eat my snack or meal anyway because it's the next right thing.

When I want to exercise more, I don't because it's the next right thing.

I don't particularly appreciate that these are the next right thing, so, for now, I'll act robotically in the hopes that these changes will eventually become the norm.

My eating disorder's method of encouragement during stress is to tell me not to eat. It has become so familiar I don't recognize it and act upon it again and again. I am slowly breaking the cycle.

Doing the next right thing is my ticket to recovering from ED.

Your Turn

How do you tell ED to leave you alone?

Do you tell ED to leave you alone, or do you succumb to its wishes?

Have you ever told ED to leave you alone?

If so, how did it feel?

I'm guessing it wasn't easy. But yay for you!

How do you stop yourself from automatically engaging in self-destructive behaviors?

What can you do to help yourself in those moments so that you can do the next right thing?

It might merely be reminding yourself or posting sticky notes all over your house, on the dashboard in your car, etc., which read, "Do the next right thing."

Jet Airways

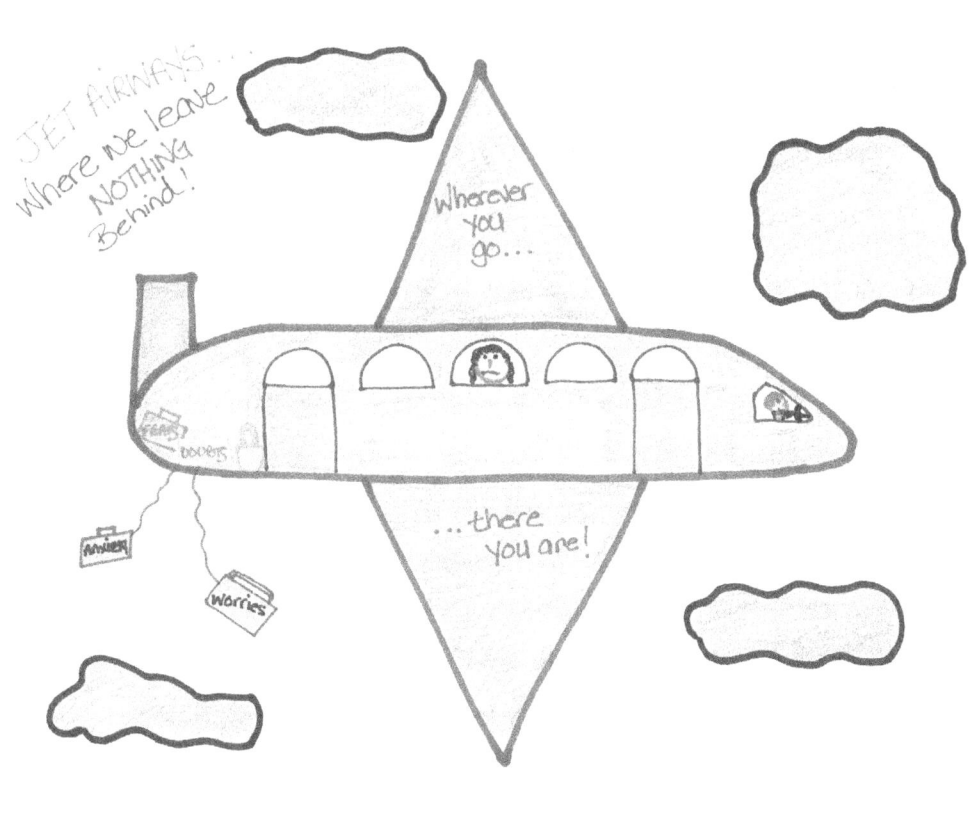

My Turn

I often feel like I want to get away from it all.

When I get the urge to run, sometimes literally, the realization hits me that wherever I go, there I am. I can't escape myself, no matter how hard I try.

The bottom line is I need a mental recess from myself and others. It's not selfish to give myself one either. There's nothing wrong with taking a break from people, places, and situations. As long as I'm not harming myself or others or avoiding my feelings by doing so, then I'm allowed a turn.

Toddlers and preschoolers get naps, working adults get lunch breaks, and college students get a few weeks off between semesters.

With that being the case, who says I don't deserve a breather, especially when my brain works on overdrive 24 hours a day, 365 days a year?

Your Turn

Take a break, but, and I mean this, take yourself with you and discover you aren't such bad company.

How will you take this break?

Will you spend it with someone or by yourself?

Will you explore nature, take a bath, listen to music, plant something?

Make sure you do something you enjoy. Learning to have fun again is exciting. Think of it as an adventure. It also gives us something to look back on during rough patches to remind ourselves we can push through. Plus, we get more unforgettable moments.

Life Is Like The Weather

My Turn

I remember seeing the movie *Parenthood* with Steve Martin. Helen Shaw, who played the grandma, spoke about life being like a roller coaster. She explained that a merry-go-round merely goes round and round, whereas a roller coaster brings more variety.

Life would be easy if it were a merry-go-round, and I knew what to expect, but then where would the excitement be?

The quote is so powerful I used it in one of my romance novels to make a point.

Each day brings ups, downs, twists, and turns, and I must face them head-on. It's what gives me strength and connects me to others.

During treatment, there was a morning I meditated on the rug in my family room. There I was, relaxing with spa music, when out of nowhere, my two older children began talking, and my youngest sat next to me. Add in two of our dogs playing and jumping over me as I lay on the floor. I told myself, "Amid the chaos, I am at peace."

Need I say more?

I drew a picture with those words and posted it on my dresser's mirror in my bedroom.

There will always be chaos. It's how I react to it that's important.

Your Turn

How do you react when something unexpected happens?

Can you take personal responsibility for your behavior rather than blaming outside factors?

My kids and dogs disrupting my meditation is a perfect example. I was engaging in self-care and got interrupted. I could have reprimanded my kids, but I didn't. The lesson was looking within. If I had set boundaries, informing them that when I'm meditating, they have to wait until I'm finished before engaging in conversations next to me, I wouldn't have been disturbed.

As far as the dogs, they play where and when they want to. Again, I could have set a boundary by putting them in another room or the yard.

Often, looking at my behavior and changing it will lessen over-reactivity to events outside myself. If I don't take personal responsibility, there will never be growth. Blaming others is futile.

We can only change ourselves. Focusing on changing others is useless and won't heal us. Changing ourselves will.

FUN

My Turn

A three-letter word, which means something so BIG. Without joy, why live? Yet, living in an anxiety-ridden prison is no picnic.

I take pleasure in doing things my kids and I enjoy. Some alone, some together. The obstacle I face is permitting myself to take a break and allowing myself to be present when I do. It goes along with the principle of giving myself a breather.

I don't have to psychoanalyze and therapize every act I take. It's okay to have fun for the sake of having fun.

Your Turn

You are allowed to have fun too. We all are.

What is one thing you have wanted to do, accomplish, or try but haven't for whatever reason?

Today is the day.

Live your life.

Don't wait for it to happen.

Make it happen.

If the thing you want to achieve or do is unobtainable or out of reach, at least take a step toward it. Losing weight or looking a certain way doesn't count. Those are ED's goals, not ours.

****

Add-on during editing.

My dream was to become a published author.

With my first romance trilogy written, I submitted book one to various publishers. Multiple rejections crushed my hope. I didn't give up, though. I had made up my mind that the three books would get published and put that energy into the universe.

A few editors gave me constructive feedback and suggestions. In particular, one said if I incorporated her ideas, she would take another look at my manuscript.

It took about a month of research and revisions, but I did the footwork.

Not only did the publisher accept the first manuscript, but they also agreed to publish books two and three.

Fear and self-doubt crept in. How would I put these books out there for the world to see—I mean, read? They contain sexual content. What if people viewed me in a different light because of my genre, contemporary romance with spice?

I read a saying that I have since taped next to my desk. It says, "A goal without a deadline is just a dream."

How valid these words are. Whenever I postpone or procrastinate, there is usually fear behind it.

I pushed through, letting my walls down in the process. My first trilogy got published. And here, my dream had been to publish one book.

Meanwhile, several months later, my publisher closed its doors, which left me in a bind.

Stubborn, I am. I don't give up easily.

Self-publishing was my next venture, and I haven't looked back. I am now eight novels in and counting.

My reason for sharing this story is not to boast. It's to demonstrate that we're wrong when we tell ourselves we can't do something. We can. It may take perseverance, dedication, and a ton of hard work, but goals are doable and achievable, just like recovery is.

So, I pose the question again, what is one thing you have wanted to do, accomplish, or try but haven't for whatever reason?

The dedication in my first novel reads: For those who don't believe dreams come true. They can, and they do.

If I can make my dream come true with all of my anxiety and ED's ugly voice roaring in the background, so can you!

To-Do List

My Turn

It's easy to get caught up in the "I need to..." and "I should..." voices in my head.

Seeing the list on paper makes it less daunting. Crossing off things that aren't emergent makes the tasks more doable.

I do the same with the shoulds—scratch off tasks that aren't of great significance.

Looking at what's left, I prioritize the first three items.

As I've said in previous entries, in my perfectionistic mind, every task has equal importance. By proving I can do it all, it boosts my worthiness of love and acceptance.

Being a people-pleaser has made me a nervous wreck. Other people live their lives, la-di-da, while I work nonstop. Anger and resentment set in as a result.

Doing things outside myself to fill me doesn't work. How many times have I purchased shoes or a new outfit, felt the rush of buying them, only to lose the excitement after wearing them?

It goes back to looking within. It is there where I get the natural high I can build and grow upon.

Your Turn

Write a to-do list.

What three things must get done, for example, paying the electric bill?

Nourishing your mind and body should always be numero uno. That's a given, so list it above the top three.

What shoulds can wait?

Can someone assist with some of the items on the list?

I hate asking for help but am s...l...o...w...l...y learning to.

Don't forget to add self-care to the list. It's both a must and a should.

You Found Me

My Turn

Playing is something I don't do enough of—playing games with my kids, playing with the dogs.

Guilt pokes at me and tells me I'm not giving quality attention to my children. When in reality, I over-give to each of them.

On a different note, I'm doing my kids an injustice by doing everything for them. They must learn to take responsibility for their actions and behaviors, the same as I do.

My days consist of chores, work, administrative tasks, writing, and so on. There isn't much room left to play with my kids.

This past weekend, I took my daughter to a movie, just the two of us, and it was awesome. I also did arts and crafts with my youngest. Quality moments like these are what stand out to me the most, and I'm sure to my kids too.

As a child, my mother did everything for me and tried to fix every problem. She did it out of love, but unfortunately, it left me in a mindful jail with a false belief that I'm incapable of handling crises.

The reality is, I'm highly responsible, respectable, and capable. I don't want my children to live a life filled with the same doubts I grew up with. Self-sufficiency as an adult is crucial.

Letting go is essential for them to achieve that. Having fun with them doesn't hurt either. I make sure we have loads of it.

Your Turn

Do you feel all work and no play makes for a dull life?

Are you allowing yourself periods to play and have fun?

How does doing these things make you feel?

Do you believe you deserve to take time for yourself—that breather principle again?

If not, what will it take to change your mind?

If you do, keep it up!

What is one nice thing you can do for yourself?

It doesn't have to be big. It can be as simple as watching your favorite TV show or doodling.

Be creative. That's how I discovered how much I enjoy drawing.

Drama In Your Life

My Turn

I spoke with a former patient from treatment—the previously mentioned patient with the pessimistic attitude in the Now Playing entry—that I distanced myself from. I'm trying to walk the bumpy road of recovery and see her stuck in quicksand. Her negativity adversely affects me. Additionally, listening to her cycle of drama reinforced that I no longer want to live in that place.

I found myself in a better mood after hearing about her misery. It sounds selfish, but her words provided me with insight.

She is the perfect example of the type of person I don't want to be, a role model for perpetual sickness. She said she had lost hope to recover even though she had been in recovery for years prior to her relapse. Ongoing treatment has become her way of life, enabling her to benefit from staying sick.

I don't want to be in treatment again. I have been there and done that. Once for anxiety and once for ED. Both experiences gave me tools.

Recognizing the drama in my life—what separates the musicals from the tragedies—has been significant in distinguishing what's meaningful versus superficial bullshit that no longer warrants my attention.

I prefer to live in a musical where people are happy and sing through life.

I try to surround myself with spiritual people. I can't save everyone or be everybody's therapist, which my codependent self loves to do.

There will be all kinds of people in different recovery stages along my path, and I will learn from every one of them. Still, I must respect where I'm at and not get dragged in the mud with others who do not make sound decisions for themselves.

Your Turn

Do you find yourself trying to rescue others?

Do certain people in your life bring you up, whereas others bring you down?

There was some guilt involved when I distanced myself from the person mentioned in the entry because I didn't want to offend her. However, the relationship was unhealthy and triggered ED's voice; therefore, it had to be done.

Have you ever put your needs aside out of fear of upsetting someone?

Did you end up getting hurt?

Is it evident that drama seekers usually only talk about themselves and rarely ask or care much about what's happening in your life?

When it comes to the people in your life, who are the role models?

What can you do to take care of yourself and surround yourself with them?

Hint: Boundary setting.

Our recovery has to be a priority over anyone else's, whether others call us selfish or not.

We come first.

If someone is affecting our recovery or dragging us down, we must release them, even if only temporarily. Misery loves company. ED loves misery.

Cookie Jar

My Turn

My older son blamed me for something I had nothing to do with, and I laughed.

He didn't.

I explained the importance of taking responsibility for our actions.

The situation reminded me of a nursery rhyme about stealing cookies from a cookie jar. It's so easy to say, "I didn't do it," and blame somebody else.

Taking personal responsibility is hard. So is recovery. But blaming others and manipulating eats me up inside. They are blinding tactics that keep me sick.

****

Add-on during editing.

I no longer blame others, thanks to years of hard work.

Manipulating situations to work in my favor is something I remind myself not to do. It involves converting others to my views.

Inner calm grows when I make well-thought-out decisions that don't mislead or sway others.

Your Turn

In what ways does manipulating and blaming serve you?

ED tells us they do, which subsequently gives it more power over us.

How will ED try to make you feel if you take personal responsibility since doing the right thing goes against everything it stands for?

For me, it means being honest about my meal plan, even when I don't follow it. It also means taking responsibility for other harmful behaviors, such as over-exercise, because keeping ED's secrets only makes it stronger.

We must be honest with ourselves and others. Lying or manipulating on ED's behalf is self-defeating. It no longer deserves to be protected. Not that it ever did.

Boxing

My Turn

The topic at my weekly group was about treating friends the way we treat ourselves. The consensus was we would never treat friends as harshly as we treat ourselves.

Why do I beat myself up over things I don't do right yet encourage my friends with positive feedback or advice?

Why can I give words of praise to others but not to myself?

Why is it I only want what's best for others yet put myself down?

Why is it okay to disrespect myself?

Where did this idea that I deserve to live in mental confinement with fear and doubt somehow manifest itself into my believing it's acceptable?

It's not.

In my group, the facilitators tell us we deserve good things. I have to remind myself about this often. I deserve the same level of kindness I offer to others. The sad reality is it's easier to give it to others than to myself.

Your Turn

Do you beat up on yourself?

Do you treat yourself the way you treat others?

In what ways can you start being gentler with yourself?

Is it possible to treat yourself the way you would treat a loved one, such as your inner child, who deserves an abundance of love?

*****

Add-on during editing.

Treating myself with the same compassion I treat my family with was a foreign concept to me.

I still get frustrated with myself but to a much lesser degree, depending on the circumstance.

Although I'm not fond of making mistakes—once a perfectionist, always a perfectionist—I can accept when I make them.

Working on mindfulness has helped me tremendously. Accepting being imperfect has been a blessing.

My growth has come in steps so small they are microscopic. I am a work in progress and continue to learn daily.

Recognizing powerlessness and letting go have been instrumental in releasing some of the control I never had to begin with.

My recovery has been a culmination of practicing various tools and strategies, falling, getting up, relapsing, and doing the next right thing. Repeat. The journey is eternal, which, in my view, is a benefit. I don't have to pressure myself to get to the finish line by a certain date.

Deepening my spirituality keeps me hopeful and gives me strength, especially when it feels like life is falling apart around me.

Filling Your Tank

My Turn

I remember a therapist telling me to add the word "but" when something upsetting happens. For example, I unpacked my daughter's suitcases from sleep-away camp and dropped a heavy bottle on my baby toe.

Ouch!

After a few curse words, I told my daughter I needed a time out and retreated to my office to work on one of my romance novels.

Once in a calmer state, I re-evaluated the event and added the word "but."

I dropped the heavy bottle, *but* I didn't blame my daughter or yell at her.

My toe was in pain, *but* I had an energy healing workshop scheduled that I couldn't wait to attend the following afternoon.

Adding in this simple word made a huge difference in both my attitude and perspective.

Your Turn

Which fuel will you add to your tank, positive or negative?

Even in the worst situations, our attitudes and how we perceive events make all the difference. It affects how we react to them.

What kind of day do you want to have?

****

Add-on during editing.

Today I use the phrase "It could always be worse," rather than "but." When things don't go as planned, more often than not, I look at the bigger picture because, in reality, things could always be worse.

Keeping this at the forefront of my mind has been fundamental in keeping things in perspective and dealing with them. I have said the words often enough that they have become ingrained.

Try it out. If my words don't float your boat, come up with an encouraging saying of your own.

Christian Grey

My Turn

My therapist gave me the assignment to do something I like since I haven't in weeks, possibly months. I have lost the thrill to work on my romance novels—writer's block.

My husband suggested I read *Fifty Shades of Grey* by E.L. James. I had heard mixed reviews but decided why not?

Who would've ever imagined the series would become a coping tool for ED? I kid you not. I read the entire trilogy in less than a month. It became my go-to, rather than exercise, when I needed a break.

It gave me a heavenly escape from the craziness I call life. Reading the trilogy inspired me to draw again as well as continue working on my romance novels.

The excitement of entering Christian's Red Room of Pain—in the book, of course—gave me something to look forward to—an out—that didn't focus on food or exercise.

Your Turn

I offer you the same assignment my therapist gave me. Do something for yourself.

You might ask, "Like what? I don't even know what I like."

That's fine. It gives you the perfect opportunity to explore new interests.

A Posse Of One

My Turn

I have joked that my scattered mind is like Sybil's. Those who don't know who she is, look up Sally Field with Sybil's name and discover a gem.

The committee in my head tells me how to behave, what to think, what so and so thinks of me, what I need to do, and so on.

I've lost touch with the idea that ED is trying to harm me and isn't who I am as a person. It's the self-destructive part of me. There are also parts of me who love to read, draw, write, sing, and do other creative things.

This week I'm cluing into ED's voice and acutely listening to how it tells me to behave and respond to life's gifts, as I shall so earnestly call them.

Ironically, this recognition is helping me ignore ED and not take its advice.

ED is pissed. It will shout to get my attention, annoyingly loud too.

Listening and distinguishing ED's voice from my own is vital. It provides me with an option to refocus and choose an alternate path when unpleasant situations arise. I'm consciously listening to my voice of reason.

I'm full of many thoughts, feelings, and beliefs. I'm not any one of them in isolation but a culmination of all of them. I didn't learn poor coping skills overnight, so I can't expect to get rid of them that quickly either.

Being with ED is like driving a car with no brakes. The ride can't stop. But if it were a car like one in *The Flintstones*, I could put my foot down and save myself from the inevitable crash ED wants me to get into—one with a disastrous outcome.

Nobody can put their foot down on my behalf. It's my job. The issue arises that being alone in my head is what got me into this mess. Compassion from others is a necessity.

I never tell anyone when ED is driving. There's a silent plea to protect it. What would I do if someone took ED away from me?

Recover, perhaps?

It comes back to the idea that I'm the only one who can put my foot down against ED.

Your Turn

Who's driving your car?

If it's ED, can you shove it aside? Better yet, toss it out the window and climb into the driver's seat?

If the answer is no, why not?

If you're afraid to drive alone, can you ask someone to take the ride with you?

Hint: Ask for support.

What does ED's voice sound like today?

Is it a whisper?

Is it blasting?

Is it lurking in the distance, waiting to pounce and attack?

Imagine ED is a person you want nothing to do with because hate resides inside it. Get behind the wheel and drive in the opposite direction ED wants you to go in.

Above The Line

My Turn

I went to a parenting workshop at my kids' school and was blown away by the information presented.

To preface, the school follows the philosophy of Dr. Gardner's Multiple Intelligence Theory, which, simply put, means we have multiple intelligences, not solely I.Q.

The principal holds monthly coffee talks that I regularly attend because I find her lectures inspirational. She is the mother of a physically disadvantaged son and has an incredible outlook and attitude.

All year she has spoken to the parents about living above the line. This concept comes from the authors of *Top 20 Training*, whom she brought to talk to us.

In a nutshell, we learned two things:

1. We can look at things with an open mind—a framework where we are receptive to learning from situations around us,
or
2. We can choose to blame and point fingers at others for everything wrong in our lives—both within and outside of us.

Where am I today, above or below the line?

At my support group, a woman spoke about the difficulty she was having with ED. She had been struggling for weeks.

I mentioned what I'd learned. When we are above the line, we see things for what they are, whereas when we are below the line, almost everything seems bleak.

It's all about perspective.

I've been trying to look at things from a different angle because mine is usually one-sided, meaning I want to see things my way, period.

By being open-minded, I am willing to hear various viewpoints. I have even gone so far as changing mine when they aren't in my best interest, as rough as it may be.

Overscheduling myself is usually a black and white area for me. I'm going back to basics and using my husband's suggestion of prioritizing tasks. How easily I forget to apply newly learned skills.

As I've said, there will always be unplanned obstacles, like my husband calling from work to inform me one of our employees had to leave early, which meant he needed me at the office pronto.

These forks in the road that alter my rigid schedules throw me for a loop.

I'm working on my inner dialogue and trying to remain above the line. It isn't easy, but I see a difference already. I have less angst and am getting more things done.

Your Turn

What type of glasses are you wearing?

Are they blinders, which make you only see in front of you?

Bifocals, where you have to balance above but fall slightly below the line?

How about contacts, where there are no obstructions, and you can see all around you?

What can you do to wear contact lenses today?

How can you view things differently to see them in a brighter light?

What can you do to make that a reality?

Do it!

I Have No Patience

My Turn

The framework from which I see life is overwhelming and scary. The parenting workshop I attended, mentioned in the Above The Line entry, tells me it doesn't have to be. I can reframe my thoughts, which, as a result, will make life more enjoyable.

I've been in therapy for years. You name the style, and I've tried it. Even during treatment, the therapists stressed the importance of changing my thinking.

There are times I'm more amenable to change than others. Presently, I'm in an open phase.

Hearing what the researchers discussed at the workshop coincides with what multiple therapists, self-help books, and TV shows have told me. Perhaps it was meant to be for me to hear the lesson again, phrased differently.

The researchers and authors of *Top 20 Parents* discussed a TLC approach, which means thinking, learning, and communicating.

Me, communicate, and use my voice? They had to be joking.

Seriously though, I must modify how I think about something when my way doesn't work. This confusion or stuckness can be inspiring, as long as I push through it and get to the "aha!" moment instead of giving up because things get too hard.

It's easier to throw in the towel and fall into old patterns than to learn something that takes conscious effort. Changing my thoughts is HARD. They are what I know. They are what I'm used to.

Making the necessary changes can take on the same probability as walking on water, which is unobtainable and impossible. It would be easier to stay stuck in anxiety and depression than have to put in so much effort.

****

Add-on during editing.

Reframing my thoughts means looking at a situation differently and learning in the process.

The researchers stressed how great mistakes are. They are what lead to growth and transformation.

Such a relief to hear.

I have always been under the assumption that if I did something wrong, others would reject me.

Being a perfectionist means I become a punching bag when I don't cross a t or dot an i.

The choice to view a situation differently is mine to make.

The other morning I was premenstrual and moody, and my husband was lovey-dovey.

Instead of communicating to him that my lack of desire had nothing to do with him, I put on my bitch suit, only to feel horrible about my poor behavior.

I later spoke to him, sans the bitch suit. After sharing that my foul mood had everything to do with my hormones, he understood where I was coming from.

I *assumed* he knew how I was feeling. He *assumed* I didn't want to be lovey-dovey with him.

Both of us were wrong. It was poor communication on both of our parts.

My daughter's computer wouldn't turn on. I told my husband I might have accidentally unplugged it when I cleaned the floor. Of course, I said it through gritted teeth because I was afraid to get "in trouble" even though logically, I knew I wouldn't. This fear stems from my childhood, where my sisters and I got reprimanded for the silliest mistakes.

I am changing that pattern. Shit happens. Oh well. C'est la vie.

The computer got fixed, and it was no big deal.

Your Turn

Think back to a recent mistake, big or little. How did it make you feel afterward?

What did you tell yourself?

If the words were uplifting, good for you. If they weren't, write about the mistake and how you could reframe your reaction to it.

Could you look at it from someone else's perspective or standpoint—not a past abuser—picture someone loving and kind?

What assumptions were you making, or what were others possibly making about you?

What lesson can be learned from this?

How likely is it that this new awareness will prevent you from making the same mistake?

If it's improbable, write alternative views and actions, even if you find them foolish, that you could take, which would lead you to an "aha" moment rather than an ED moment.

Put at least one of these into practice. Please make sure they are realistic alternatives.

Recovery Bank

My Turn

ED behaviors discussed. Read with caution.

Last week at my support group, I shared about not seeing any consequences of ED and got a wake-up call regarding tough love. Group members said in so many words I was in denial.

Cringeworthy.

I hated being the center of attention, especially when others were calling me out.

A woman who had been in recovery and returned from another stint in long-term treatment jumped into the conversation. She informed us about her health issues as a result of ED. Seeing her, you would never know she had medical problems, which was her point in telling us.

It brought to life the idea that you don't have to look the part of having an eating disorder to suffer from its detrimental effects.

This insight has kept me on my toes. I look in the mirror and see a healthy appearance, yet I don't know what damage I've done to my organs. It's terrifying.

I want to be in top form from the inside out. It's so darn hard when ED tricks me into thinking otherwise. Piece of shit, ED!

My therapist asked me to make one small change—just one. Like I haven't been told that before.

One of the group facilitators talked about making deposits in our recovery account and writing them in a check register. With my register in hand, I'm ready to accumulate deposits and jot down new practices.

The deposits are risks and challenges I take to fight against ED. By writing them down, I can see my progress; otherwise, they get quickly forgotten. Plus, without having a visual, it becomes easier to focus on mistakes rather than accomplishments.

There can be no withdrawals from this account. It's a savings account only. It's a treasure of deeds done well, decisions done right, battles fought, and words spoken.

Here are my deposits so far:

Friday: I sat at the kitchen table and ate lunch. While doing so, the committee in my head told me to put clothes in the dryer, put dishes away, and so forth.

I forced myself to remain glued to the chair.

I talked to my sister on the phone but didn't mention how difficult it was to eat in peace.

It was evident from this experience that I don't discuss the tension that arises during meals. It also revealed I'm always on the move. It's a learned behavior and scores points for ED.

I was excited about my achievement.

Saturday: My in-laws came to visit, and I took the opportunity to work on my romance novel while they played with my younger son, daughter, and husband in the pool.

I usually come up with excuses to keep me from engaging in a self-satisfying activity. Instead, I chose to write because it makes me happy.

Sunday: My husband asked me to swim with him and our youngest child in the morning when I usually exercise. I hesitatingly agreed because I wanted to have fun with them. The problem was ED told me differently.

I swam some laps and played in the pool. I told myself it's beneficial to switch up types of physical activity. Of course, ED had its say. It said to do more, that playing in the pool wasn't enough. I acknowledged its comments and chose to disagree.

It wasn't easy, and ED was insistent and persistent throughout the rest of the day with its urges. I kept saying, "No."

My husband and I then went to a movie. After, he recommended we go for frozen yogurt. I denied his request. He asked who was making the decision, me or ED. I told him the truth. In response, he drove us to the yogurt shop.

While there, I made a "safe" choice. I took it as a win because I ate the frozen yogurt. I even added a topping, and it was yummy. My husband and I had fun. ED didn't.

These are examples of my deposits so far.

Seeing them in a journal, check register, notebook, phone, etc., brings them to life. When ED is rowing the boat, I can review these victories and know I have succeeded in the past, which means I can do so again.

****

My therapist gave me a suggestion. I'm getting a lot of them this week. She told me that in 20 minutes, she heard me say the word "can't" four or five times—a term I tell my kids not to use. I didn't realize I said it so often.

She told me to listen when I say it and replace it with the word "choose." When I tell myself I can't do something, I'm *choosing* not to do it. The shift in focus from "I can't" to "I choose not to" gives me power over my decisions.

Your Turn

Grab a notebook and pen, laptop, or phone, and create your register for the week. Only good stuff can go into it, big or small. All successes count and add up.

The deposits might fluctuate. I had two deposits on Sunday, and on others, only one.

The important thing is to keep adding to your bank of recovery.

Do you find you also say "I can't" a lot?

Can you replace it with "I choose not to" instead?

Try it out and see how it feels.

Balance Of Hope

My Turn

Why am I full of hope on some days, and others feel the war against ED is too hard to fight?

Why is it I know what the right thing to do is logically yet choose not to do it?

Why do I assume I am different from everyone else, and there's no solution for the excessive amount of anxiety I carry around with me?

Why do I keep my emotions locked securely in a gun safe so nobody can get to them?

How is it I can feel alone in my house when my husband, kids, and pets are inside it.

How is it an eating disorder blindsided me?

I continue to search for the answers. Often, I keep my mind so busy that it prevents me from deepening my spiritual outlook to the extent needed to get them.

I am an isolationist who hates being alone.

Isn't that ironic?

I long for connections with others but am overly selective in who I connect with. That has caused me to miss out on many opportunities throughout my life. After all, nobody feels the way I do. I purposely say this because if I were the only person who felt this way, there wouldn't be other attendees at my support group, and I would've been the sole patient in treatment.

This knowledge transforms despair into hope.

When I hear others speak at my weekly group and ten other women raise their hands because they identify, it gives me hope.

When my husband points out healthy changes, it gives me hope.

When my therapist tells me I worked hard during a session, it gives me hope.

When I face a challenge and walk through it, it gives me hope.

When I step out of my comfort zone, it gives me hope.

Every inch forward in recovery brings me hope. It means I know there's something better, and I'm willing to reach for it.

Your Turn

Taking risks and handling change doesn't come easily, but neither is living with ED.

Is living with ED easy for you?

If your answer is yes, ED is reading this book instead of you, and you can tell it to get lost. You wouldn't be reading it in the hopes there is something better out there if a part of you didn't believe it.

Where are you on the balance scale of hope?

Are you hopeful and optimistic?

Write about it. It will be a treasure to refer to when you're in a slump.

On the other hand, are you feeling hopeless?

What's causing this attitude?

Write about it.

Read over what you wrote and see if fear is a primary factor behind your hopelessness.

What can you do to modify a situation you perceive as bad?

Situations, like feelings, as I've mentioned, are neither good nor bad. Some are simply better than others.

If I had healthier coping skills, I wouldn't be writing a book about suffering from an anxiety disorder and ED. I don't say these words lightly. I understand the imbalance of being hopeful and hopeless and how the two oscillate.

We are on this journey together.

Section IX
Wrapping It Up... Or Am I?
What's Inside The Windows?

My Turn

My therapist gave me a homework assignment to draw a picture with windows. Each window had to have a person or circumstance inside it that causes me undue stress.

Behind the curtain of the first window is my sister, who has cut me out of her life.

Losing a sibling who is alive is almost worse than losing one permanently. When one passes, we go through the stages of grief and move forward. Of course, suffering a loss isn't as simple as that. It's excruciatingly painful and takes a long time to recover from, if ever.

Losing a person who is alive is a double whammy. It's like having to go through the grieving process twice.

Since my father's funeral, there has been no communication between one of my sisters and me. This particular sister—the middle one, number three— is not speaking to the one directly above me in age—number four—either.

Sister number four sent a caring text to sister number three. The response was, "I don't know who this message is from. Don't ever contact me again."

My middle sister knew exactly who the text was from based on the message sent and the phone number.

Such a tragedy. It cuts deep. It's the realization my sister doesn't want anything to do with us.

If my own flesh and blood can toss me aside like a piece of garbage, why would I trust others won't do the same?

And therein lie my adult child of an alcoholic's trust issues.

At first, I felt anger. I then went back and forth through the grieving stages. It wasn't easy since I was also mourning the loss of my father.

It progressed to sadness with an understanding that my sister is working from the only place she knows—an adult child of an alcoholic who never sought emotional support. Her inner pain and suffering, along with her absence from my life, are heartrending.

I have many tools to use regarding the acceptance of what is and letting go. They are my new reality. I can't control my sister's decisions, actions, or emotions. Still, I am a person with feelings. Underneath my understanding and acceptance is where the pain lies. And it hurts.

Window Number Two: Mom

My mother is preoccupied with getting her will organized. I tell her it upsets me when she brings it up. That I would rather have her in my life than any material item she leaves behind.

The truth is, at some point, I won't have her anymore. That reality is tearing me up inside.

We know as kids, one day, our parents will no longer be with us. As I get older, so does my mother, and it frightens me to no end.

I've already been through the process of losing one parent. It took a lot of inner work to have unconditional love with no residual anger toward my father before he passed. I've been working on the same type of forgiveness for my mother. She's loving and caring. The thing is, she was a workaholic. I suffer a great deal of emotional abandonment from both of my parents. It's something that arises and interferes when building new relationships. Hence, I usually choose to avoid doing so altogether.

My mother did the best she could with her skillset, the same as my dad did.

My sisters and I are a product of the coping skills our parents brought into their marriage. I'll admit there were many useful ones.

The fear of losing my mother is overwhelming. It is codependency multiplied by ten. In a life where I often feel alone, my mom and husband are my two constants who always support me without judgment. I also have my children and a few close friends, but these relationships aren't the same as a mother/daughter relationship.

Logic doesn't take away heartache. My mind and heart are separate. I have a great outlook. I'm more spiritual and accepting than ever before, but my heart is full of pain. Pain from a loss I haven't suffered yet. Pain, I know, is inevitable.

I recently finished the 8-week Mindfulness-Based Stress Reduction Course. To keep true to the program's teachings, I should be living in the moment, accepting that I have thoughts about losing my mother, acknowledging them, but not following that trail of thinking to a dark place.

Distracting myself, breathing, and nonjudgmentally experiencing my feelings are excellent coping tools. The thing is, my emotions are still there. I'm not going to pretend they don't exist.

Mindfulness tells me to accept my feelings for what they are.

Okay. If that's the case, I'm sad about this particular situation. This sadness goes past my heart and into the pit of my stomach. It's always with me, glued to the walls of my heart and intestines.

The purpose of this assignment was to delve deeper into my feelings. As I write this, I'm sad, tears are flowing, and my heart and stomach ache.

Mission accomplished on my therapist's part.

Window Number Three: Dad

This brings me to the next window, my dad. I miss seeing him at the memory care center. He may have been in a horrible state of Alzheimer's, but he always looked happy to see me. His entire face would light up.

It's hard to acknowledge that I'll never see him smile again.

The losses I've experienced, and the fear of future losses, are what's keeping me stuck with one foot in and one foot out of ED. Thankfully, I'm in a better place than when I reentered treatment—more about that in the next section.

Window Number Four: Me

This week has been brutal. I turn 51 on Monday. I'm at a midpoint— contemplating life, where I've been, where I'm going, and who I am. Philosophical stuff mostly.

I'm enrolled in different online classes to learn about myself and feed my spirit. I'm attending my codependency meetings, have a sponsor, and am working the Twelve Steps.

Yet here I sit, with sadness.

Writing romance novels has filled me in a way nothing else has. My books become my children. I create characters, build them, nurture them, give them human feelings and realistic situations to confront and deal with, then set them free. The best part is they are my babies.

The items listed above bring me joy.

The only holes that remain are the holes of loss. I can pad them with the healthier coping skills I'm developing, but the holes are craters. They are permanent scars.

I'm hoping all the skills I've learned, and practice will eventually get me out of the holes of sadness faster without allowing ED to push me back into them.

That said, ED has gotten louder this week, and isolation has set in.

"I'm fine," I tell everyone.

I'm not fine.

My husband commented a week ago that he sees me grasping at anything to make me feel better. He referred to all the classes I'm taking, which add to my daily responsibilities of work, the house, the kids, the dogs, the bills, etc.

He's right. I'm grasping. I'm tired of feeling stuck, anxious ALL the time, having panic attacks, doing everything for everyone, not using my voice as often as I should, and being kind and thoughtful to everyone except myself.

Maybe there's a reason my name is Faith.

I have it.

It's what keeps me going.

It's what keeps me searching for answers.

Fortunately, my current search involves looking within.

Your Turn

If you had to draw windows and put the people, places, and things inside them that cause you undue stress and emotional grief, who/what would they be?

You can list them. They don't have to be drawn.

Once you have the main items, explore what arises, and write about it.

If this exercise is too painful because of past trauma, you might want to make a list but share what comes up with a therapist or trained professional.

I did my journaling at home then processed the information with my therapist. The mindset I was in had me emotionally safe enough to explore the feelings independently.

It's important not to force yourself to go to a dark place you're not ready to visit. Some situations need the assistance of a professional to guide you through them. Only you know what's emotionally safe for you.

Miss You, Dad

My Turn

On February 18th, I will be celebrating my 25th wedding anniversary. It seemed like yesterday when my husband and I met at a party, he went to his car in the rain to get an umbrella, brought it to me, then walked me to my car so that I wouldn't get wet. Swoon-worthy. I knew he was a keeper.

It also happens to be the anniversary of my dad's passing—two years.

Last year my husband and I visited my father at the cemetery. It was hard. My husband comforted me. I know he's upset that all future anniversaries will bring up memories of my dad.

During the first year of grieving, I wrote another romance novel and used my father's experience at the residential Alzheimer's center as the basis for the storyline. I wanted to release the book last year but couldn't. The pain was still too great. I set the book aside.

This year I made it my mission to release the novel on my anniversary. The book is dedicated to my father and entitled, *Remember Me*. I feel a sense of relief and closure. I know my dad is smiling down on me.

I also decided to move forward with this workbook and put my shame about ED aside. My father helped many people while attending Alcoholics Anonymous. He saved lives. He was an inspiration, a spiritual man with a heart of gold.

If I told my past self that I would write loving words of praise about my father one day, it would have told me I was joking because my inner child had too much rage.

She no longer does.

This workbook is dedicated to my father as well—both parents. He taught me the importance of being a kind and honest person. He also taught me the importance of living a spiritual life. I do so to the best of my ability.

I may have had a rough start during my childhood years, which manifested into severe anxiety and panic during my teen years and onward, but I can finally say I'm at a place of acceptance with it.

This is who I am, a loving person who is sensitive and empathetic to others. These traits connect me to people on a level many don't get to visit.

When I drew the picture of my parents and me with my husband on the sideline saying, "It's our anniversary," I, for sure, figured I would be sobbing. That guilt would riddle me because our 25th anniversary is a testament to the dedication we have toward each other. Interestingly enough, I wasn't.

We have been through a lifetime of events in the years we've been together. We've brought three beautiful and loving children into this world, have faced adversity, have built a business, and have encouraged each other through all of it.

I am more grateful than ever. I'm looking ahead to wearing funky sunglasses to all the incredible events I have yet to experience and am doing my thing—writing and writing some more, allowing myself to have fun, and for once, making myself a priority. Others might not like it and think I'm inconsiderate, but you know what? I don't care. I used to.

This past year has been brutal emotionally. I've peeled away layers of the onion and gotten to the core. It hasn't been easy. Many days sucked. On several, I cried. On others, I had to rest from mental exhaustion.

All the work I have put into myself, including going back to treatment, has been worth it.

You know why?

Because I'm worth it.

And you are, too.

The journey of recovery has highs and lows. I choose to pummel forward.

"Screw it. This shit is too hard," still comes to me.

ED loves that. It fills my mind with all the things it can do for me to relieve the worry. It makes all kinds of promises it can't keep.

The crazy part is I continue to buy into them. I'm not going to lie and say I don't. What I can say is I'm in a peaceful state of mind more often than not. I'll take this type of progress over perfection any day.

In the words of Dr. Shauna Shapiro, a mindfulness psychologist, I am proof that what you practice grows stronger.

The more I practice meditating, mindfulness, energy healing, listening to inspirational speakers, writing, delving into my feelings, and exploring areas of interest, the more automatic positive thoughts become.

This workbook is the culmination of my eight years in recovery so far. It's incredible to look back and see how far I've come. The best part is I'm grateful for what lies ahead even though more work needs to be done.

By living in the moment, one day at a time, I'm ready to step into the future.

Your Turn

Recovery is continuous. We're in a perpetual state of evolving.

I hope that as you worked through the pages of this workbook, you discovered new truths about yourself, such as things you enjoy and things that no longer serve you. I also hope you were able to add new and healthier coping tools to your bag of tricks. Most importantly, I hope you realized that you deserve recovery.

List some of the skills you have found to be effective during troublesome and challenging times.

How can you integrate these newly acquired skills into your daily life, so they become automatic responses to triggering events?

If you aren't feeling it right now, no worries, this book doesn't explode when you reach the last page. Go back and work through all or some of the activities again.

It isn't a failure if you can't come up with any. The failure is tossing the book aside and telling yourself nothing can help you and that you're different from everyone else.

I used to believe that. Now I know differently. We all have feelings. Unfortunately, we didn't or don't have an effective means of coping with them.

This workbook has provided a lot of suggestions. Add more if you wish to. The list can be endless. There is no black and white thinking and no room for self-criticism.

Pat yourself on the back for getting to this page.

Every inch of self-care adds up to yards of recovery.

Let's continue to take this journey together.

Section X
Bonus Entries
(Some made during the COVID pandemic)

I'm Stuck!

My Turn

ED behaviors discussed. Read with caution.

I'm going through withdrawal. The ED voice is louder than ever. All I can think about is the food plan given to me by my nutritionist.

In past sessions, she recommended one change. Now, I'm supposed to completely alter my diet and workout routine and forward her these daily modifications. If I don't comply, I'm out a nutritionist.

I've learned over the years that recovery isn't perfect. Yet here I am in a situation where perfection is expected. That isn't too much pressure to put on somebody, especially a person who feels like a failure for not completing tasks with excellence.

I have four weeks to get this thing right. It's in a written contract. No screw-ups are allowed.

It's common for addicts and alcoholics to have slips and falls. They get up, return to their Twelve-Step meetings, and talk to their sponsors. I'm in a position where I'm not even allowed to trip. I need to either "shit or get off the pot," as my nutritionist says.

ED is consuming me. My husband said all I'm talking about are the changes I'm supposed to make, validating how much brain space ED has possessed. The voice usually behaves. It remains relatively quiet. It gives me space to do my thing.

Not anymore.

I've had two great days, food and exercise-wise. Emotionally, they've sucked.

I am sick of this contract, and it's only been three days. I don't understand how putting such high expectations on someone without human error is supposed to be motivating. As it is, I'm already ready to throw in the towel.

But I won't. I never do.

My people-pleasing is coming into play. I'm not one to disappoint others. My husband keeps telling me how great I'm doing. Does he know I exercised more than I was supposed to this morning?

No.

Will I tell him?

Yes, because I can't lie or keep secrets from him.

The scale is supposed to be used only during sessions with my nutritionist.

Sorry, Charlie, I used it once.

My lunch wasn't on the "approved" meal plan. Sure, I added a starch, which I consider a win, but my husband didn't.

No matter how much my nutritionist, husband, or anybody else who doesn't suffer from an eating disorder says they understand, they don't, and they can't. They don't live with a demon criticizing their bodies and what they put into it.

I reached out to a girl from my support group. I drew this picture of being stuck with ED. I'm writing in this journal while listening to Queen. I am crying and expressing my pain.

The result?

My stomach's upset, I'm anxious, and I want to isolate and hide behind my mask.

Again, I won't.

Tomorrow is another day to start again. I will hold on to hope and not give up. And even though I'm angry, I will persevere.

It's like I'm in the Superbowl against ED. ED's fans are telling me to leave the field, screaming violently into microphones and megaphones. The sound is piercing. The winner is a no-brainer.

Nevertheless, I will organize my defense on the starting line and play the ultimate game. It will be four long quarters. In this case, four weeks.

****

Add-on during editing.

After the four weeks were up, I decided to enter treatment. I did so after my daughter left for college.

My kids weren't aware of my second round (they now are). They know I see a specialized therapist and nutritionist, but I didn't want to burden the older two with worries about me while they were away, focusing on their studies. The younger one had enough on his plate adjusting to middle school and his sister leaving for college.

My nutritionist became preoccupied with the number on the scale as the weeks progressed to the point I, too, became preoccupied with it. Our sessions ended up causing more harm than good.

I went to a day program during the hours my younger son was in school. I still saw my private and current therapist.

This round of treatment was challenging because it determined what and how much I ate, unlike the previous center.

I remained in treatment for several weeks. What I gained was a more diverse meal plan and open-mindedness to try new things.

What I didn't gain was weight.

My husband, therapist, and nutritionist were livid. I did my part, yet my weight didn't budge. It was frustrating to no end. ED was doing a victory dance.

Before entering treatment, I had started attending Codependency Anonymous. I missed seeing the empathetic women I had grown to trust.

With the backing of my therapist, I left treatment. I also switched nutritionists to one with a softer approach.

I jumped into recovery.

The energy healing classes I took fascinated me, so I signed up for Reiki I and II and reinstituted my hypnosis certification.

Spiritual healing was the answer. I had known it all along. Now I had to do the footwork and mean it.

Being mindful and practicing the Twelve-Steps has been a game-changer. I still have anxiety to an insane degree, but my outlook is different. I'm more positive, less critical, more accepting, open-minded, forgiving, and balanced all around.

Months into incorporating these skills into my life, my weight has returned to a safe level.

How do I know this?

The scale is gone, but I feel the difference in my clothes.

Blind weigh-ins are routine during my sessions with my dietitian. It's better when I don't know what the number is.

When I first started recovery, I kept saying I never wanted to go back to treatment.

My advice is never say never.

I did go back, and I'm glad. I'll never be perfect at recovery, and that's okay. I'll accept improvement, and in that regard, I've made a ton of it.

Your Turn

What are your thoughts about treatment?

Have you been to treatment or considered it?

The program I chose fit into my schedule, which made it possible for me to be there. I found one that gave me enough time to continue working and drive my son to and from school, which are two musts on my to-do list.

I worked through issues of loss and shame.

What are the biggest lessons you learned to bring with you into daily life if you have been to treatment?

Do you have a nutritionist with whom you feel secure?

Do you have a therapist who understands ED?

I spoke about the importance of having a team who understands ED at the beginning of the workbook and want to reiterate it. Having the eyes of professionals who understand the disorder guiding me is reassuring because it's easy to lose sight of when I'm slipping. They catch it immediately and stop me from spiraling further downward.

I tend to view therapists in the same light as dating. You have to find someone with whom you are compatible. Before entering my second round of treatment, the nutritionist I saw had a teaching style that didn't match my learning style. There's nothing wrong with making changes for the right reasons.

Do you put undue pressure on yourself to be perfect at recovery?

Hint: It doesn't work.

Loss Comes In Many Forms

My Turn

ED behaviors discussed. Read with caution.

My Sister:

Being cut off from my sister, who had once been one of my closest friends, was brutal. An ugly verbal argument ensued during my father's funeral, and it severed our relationship. It was in a moment of heightened emotional turmoil and sadness.

Guilt set in afterward. I sent her a text to let her know I love her regardless of what was said. I got no response.

I reached out again on a different occasion. I got nothing.

Finally, I texted her birthday wishes. I got zip.

I've accepted she isn't ready to move forward with me in her life. Her behavior was despicable, but in my heart, I have forgiven her. I pray for her and am sad she carries so much anger inside. I can't allow myself to carry the same load. It will only weigh me down and eat me up inside.

My Dad:

The loss of my father, who I have forgiven, came out of nowhere. I only have fond, loving memories of him, which took significant work.

I came to learn and accept that my dad did the best he could, just as I'm doing the best I can with my children.

I am ever so grateful to my dad for exposing me to Twelve-Step programs because without hope, I have nothing. Without faith, I can't move forward. Finding a Higher Power of my understanding has given me both.

My Daughter:

My only daughter is leaving for college. This is another painful loss.

Before moving, she's seeking treatment for an eating disorder. I've been told I'm not to blame for it, yet how can I not feel responsible? Releasing myself of guilt is something I'm working on.

My Son:

My oldest son is finishing his last year in college. He doesn't plan to return to our hometown after he graduates.

All of my babies are growing up and moving on.

My Mom:

My widowed mother is only getting older. The codependent person I am makes this attachment especially tricky. God help me when the unavoidable happens.

My Youngest:

My youngest child is entering middle school.

Time is moving quickly. I tell myself since it does, I have to enjoy each minute because it's all I have. My mother tells me this during every phone conversation. She says at her age (88), you learn to appreciate each one.

ED:

Sadly, ED is another area of control. When everything around me seems chaotic, I can control my intake of food.

How is this serving me?

The sick part of me thinks it does. The healthy part of me, the part screaming to come out, knows if I continue to dance with ED, it will be my family who suffers a loss. And that loss will be me. For that is ED's goal, to end my internal suffering.

ED wants me to disappear, like the feelings I have hidden behind my mask. The difference is ED wants me to disappear permanently, in every sense of the word. This fear is what motivates me to fight against it.

Your Turn

What forms of loss have you suffered?

It can be emotional abandonment, physical loss, friendships, etc.

How do you handle loss?

What do you do with the feelings that arise due to it?

Do you live in the moment or the past and future?

Does living in the past serve you?

If you wrote yes, how?

Can you live in a future that hasn't arrived?

Planning doesn't count as living in the future. Living in the future refers to excessive worry and what-ifs about something that hasn't taken place yet.

Does this work for you?

As a person who lives with chronic anxiety, for me, it doesn't.

What can you do to ground yourself and be truly present with what is going on at this very moment?

Go outside and listen to birds chirping.

Feel your feet on the surface below you.

Rest your palm against your heart and tune into it beating.

Smell beautiful flowers or the laundry detergent on your shirt.

Focus on your breath as a grounding force.

Getting back into the moment brings with it a sense of calm.

Breathe into it.

Be in it for what it is.

I'm Fine

My Turn

Interestingly, I listened to a mindfulness talk on anger, and I feel an abundance of it. Of course, when anyone asks me how I'm doing, I still say, "Fine."

This anger has stripped away my patience. Sadly, it has become displaced on everything around me.

My nutritionist asked me to journal to see if I could uncover what's lying underneath it. Have I mentioned I hate feeling angry and being in the presence of others expressing it?

Tuesday was the anniversary of my father's passing. It was also my 25th wedding anniversary. I felt the need to hide my sadness because it was supposed to be a happy day for my husband and me.

When I feel sad, I retreat. I don't want to be around or talk to others.

That day was also the release of my eighth romance novel—a huge accomplishment that I didn't give myself enough credit for. The story was gut-wrenching to write and edit because real-life experience formed the basis for certain scenes.

My mother is sad. She misses my dad.

My body feels submerged with emotions, which results in a loss of appetite.

Editing this ED book brings up past issues I don't want to think about. When I read the journal entries, I find many of my opinions haven't changed.

I still feel full.

I still have too much on my plate.

I still feel overloaded with responsibilities.

I still feel everyone in my family depends on me to get tasks done.

Worries about my mother remain at the forefront of my mind.

The meditation I did this morning was about feeling my feelings without judgment. Maybe a part of me is frustrated for feeling sad, the emotion underlying the anger when I have so much to be grateful for.

The quietness in the house due to the oldest kids being at college also guts me. I miss them. It makes me anticipate my middle schooler leaving.

"Remain in the moment," I tell myself.

Love surrounds me. I receive it from my mother, my sisters (all except one), my husband, my children, and select outsiders. Yet I feel alone like I haven't found my place. I try to focus on the spiritual aspect of my being to fill that void. I get moments of inner peace and have gained a healthier perspective, but the emptiness remains. Hence, the sadness.

I can feel alone when others are around me. Lacking trust only makes matters worse. I've tried multiple times to share my truth, only to get abandoned *again*. The result is learning to say I'm fine. When I'm by myself, nobody can hurt me.

ED can and does.

Hurting my body isn't something I consciously strive to do. I am beyond grateful to be healthy, capable, and able. ED causes me to engage in self-harm. I know when I engage with ED, I am making a poor decision by listening to it. But on the flip side, I falsely believe ED soothes me when I'm dealing with frustration and sadness. It also intensifies my loneliness because the result is shame.

The more I hide, the more I can secretly engage in behaviors. The inner turmoil grows, which causes me to withdraw even more to deal with it. It creates a repetitive cycle.

My tank is empty. There is nothing left to give, and that is with meditating, listening to mindfulness lectures, and engaging in self-care.

Why do I still feel this way?

Your Turn

Do you have days you feel you are holding on by a thread—that you are using all the tools in your box, yet ED is still winning the race?

What can you do on those days to pull through?

I go through the motions, continuing with self-care until the gray cloud passes, or I work through the underlying causes by journaling, drawing, or talking to my therapist.

Anger is a primary emotion. We all feel it. I am learning to accept that it is okay to experience it. The walls won't crumble beside me if I express or feel it.

How do you deal with anger?

In what ways do you express it?

Are these harmful or beneficial to yourself and others? Explore this in greater detail.

Do you tell others everything is fine when inside it's anything but?

Is there one person (or more) you can open up to when the pain gets unbearable, and you feel like you are going to combust?

Sharing feelings helps decompress inner tension.

Saying I'm okay is the same as wearing my mask. I am a portrait of perfection. At least that's what ED tells me. It says I must try harder, handle it all, and that I'm a superwoman, so stop whining. Yet inside, I am riddled with symptoms of anxiety. I'm learning it's okay not to feel okay.

Do you believe it's okay not to feel okay?

Are you allowed to have days where you feel like crap?

They're going to happen whether we want them to or not.

How can you fight against ED on those days?

Being gentle with myself comes into play on those days. It might involve doing less, reading a pleasure book, taking a bath, or relaxing in bed. All are forms of self-care.

In ED's mind, nothing I do is ever enough. It always seeks more and pushes me beyond my limits of comfort.

We are permitted not to be fine as long as we don't stay stuck in that mindset. Remember, ED feeds on negativity. It's a breeding ground to bring it to the surface. At least for me, it is. On those days, I have to be vigilant and more in tune with its critical words to shut them down.

****

Add-on during editing.

How ironic that I'm doing a final read-through of this entry on my 26th anniversary, and it's now been three years since my dad's passing. Oddly enough, I am feeling motivated and empowered. I believe it's because this book is a continuation of my dad's mission to help others. I'm honoring him by sharing my truth in an effort to inspire others to find inner peace and self-acceptance.

I love you, Dad!

The Box

My Turn

My emotions are stuck inside. I feel like Uma Thurman in *Kill Bill II*, the scene where she's locked in a dark, stuffy coffin without air. Similar to her character, I have to escape from my box if I want to survive.

It's no wonder I can't breathe. It's the same story six years later. The "bad" feeling of anger and ever-present sadness only come out during my weekly sessions with my therapist. The rest of the week, they accumulate.

My spiritual self, Alexandra, is out of reach.

My family is on the sidelines, offering their love and support.

My husband tries to fish feelings out of me, to no avail. They remain glued to the base of my throat. Too much shame and self-doubt go along with them. I don't want to be judged by others. Why would I when I'm a master at judging myself? Any more critical views would only reinforce my self-deprecating thoughts.

Then there are my dogs, who give me unconditional love.

My mom tells me how strong I am and how much she loves me.

Yet here I remain, in a box.

To break out of it, I'm meditating and listening to affirmations. I'm writing in my journal and drawing because the build-up must release itself.

My therapist asked me to write after our last session. The following is what came up.

I can't help others if I'm sinking. The pressure of life is drowning me. How many responsibilities can one person possibly carry out? Still, I do them all with excellence and efficiency. Sure, ED is steering the car at the moment, but stuff is getting done. It always does. God forbid I disappoint someone.

Demands. Tasks. To-dos. They become overwhelming. Succumbing to ED's desires is one way to at least keep that voice at bay.

This routine isn't working, though.

My husband asked how he could support me. My therapist asked what would help me.

Great questions. I don't have the answers, though, because I feel lost at sea.

While journaling in my room, a slew of options came to me regarding how my husband could support me emotionally. I wrote the words in the form of a poem and shared them with him.

Please don't be mad if I don't do something right,

Please don't get frustrated if I say no to another bite.

Please don't lose patience or give up on me,

This battle holds me hostage, and I can't seem to break free.

Please don't make comments about bodies fat or thin,

It only feeds my eating disorder, a fight I'm struggling to win.

Please give me space to try and find my way,

But please don't make judgments when I step back or sway.

Please give me hugs and tell me you care,

Please let me know it's safe to share.

Please understand these thoughts torment and repeat,

Sometimes it's hard to get on my feet.

Please see behind the mask that I wear,

Please don't get impatient and think I don't care.

All I want is acceptance, to feel I'm enough,

Yet deep down inside, there's too much stuff:

Fear of failure	Fear of anger
Fear of imperfection	Fear of confrontation
Fear of disappointing	Fear of hurting others
Fear of making mistakes	Fear of letting others get close
Panic	Worry
Jitteriness	Racing thoughts
Stomachaches	Headaches
Fatigue	

Yeah, there's lots of it.

My inner voice says not to leave out the positives:

Creative	Empathetic	Kind-hearted
Loving	Patient	Accepting
Trustworthy	Faithful	Intelligent
Spiritual	Caring	Gentle
Soft-spoken	Dependable	Reliable
Thoughtful	Talented singer and writer	Mindful of others

My positives are internal, with no mention of body shape or size,

So then why do I believe it creates my worth, convinced by its false lies?

My eating disorder is a bully; it haunts my thoughts and dreams,

To the point I give in to silence the screams.

As a result, I'm once again the victim of a hate crime,

One incited from a sickness time after time.

Then the feelings of disappointment set in again,

A cycle of sickness I want to end.

Right now's a new minute. Tomorrow's a new day,

So I'll suit up with armor and let the authentic part of me lead the way.

ED's sick game shall continue with no end date in sight,

One thing I can assure myself is I won't go down without a fight.

Never give up.

Your Turn

All these years later, I still struggle to share what's going on inside. To my credit, I've gotten better at it than I used to be.

When you suppress your feelings, do you hear ED's voice get louder?

Does engaging in ED behaviors numb you to the same effect drugs and alcohol would?

How does this help you?

Do you find it's easier to use your voice in person versus writing, i.e., text, email, social media?

It's easier for me to write than verbally share, as I did with the poem for my husband.

List your fears.

Seeing them on paper, is there any way to face or confront some of them?

List your positive traits and qualities. We all have them.

Do they mention body size, or are they internal qualities and values?

This activity brought my positives to the forefront. They make up who I am as a person. The size and shape of my body do not.

Post your "positives" list in a visible place so you can see it often and remind yourself what a great person you are.

Basic Math

My Turn

Alone and disconnected,
Mechanisms to protect my heart.
Feeling I'm a burden or a bother,
So why let anyone be a part?

Hold the feelings tightly,
Held deep within my being.
Keeping them from those around me,
Even if letting them out might be freeing.

A bottle full of what-ifs,
Floating deep within the sea.
Holds me captive with its worry,
Refusing to set me free.

Tired and exhausted,
From the tasks I have to do.
Desiring warmth and comfort,
But I won't ask for it, it's true.

Seeking solace in things around me,
A temporary fill.
Nothing fills the void inside,
Nothing outside me ever will.

Letting hope and faith guide me,
As I get through another day.
Letting go, accepting, releasing,
As I try to find my way.

Alone and disconnected,
When will the wall disappear?
It doesn't have a chance to,
When it's built with rock-hard fear.

Your Turn

What do you do on days you feel alone and disconnected?

How long do you let yourself remain in isolation, cutting yourself off emotionally from others?

What can you do to open the door to your heart and let someone inside it?

Do you find ED's voice gets louder the longer you detach from others?

As I've said throughout this workbook, my ED screams when I put up my walls. The voices get loud enough to cause hearing loss, mainly because they bounce off the walls I've set up around me.

My therapist is my savior when I block myself off from others. She will talk me through my feelings and get to the core to figure out what need isn't getting met. The next entry, Seesaw Of Needs, describes basic needs. She might also give me homework to soften my exterior. I rely on her to decompress what I've held on to over the week. For me, it's a must to check in with her. I can bounce ideas off her, share what's in my heart, any and everything.

My dietitian isn't seen as often. She encourages me to take risks, and I set intentions to challenge myself until our next visit. She's a crucial part of my recovery.

Do you have professional support available to you?

If not, as I've suggested, check out the Help And Support Are Available section for ideas on how and where to get help.

If you have a team and have been slacking off, do you see a difference in your attitude?

Support is available in many forms. We don't have to be alone and disconnected forever. Others can and do relate. We just have to find these people and connect with them.

Seesaw Of Needs

My Turn

Instead of hearing others tell me how to feel or handle things, I would prefer they acknowledge *what* I feel.

How many times have I heard others say, "Don't be sad," or "You shouldn't let things get to you."

Thanks for sharing.

What I'd rather hear is, "That sounds difficult," or "How about a hug?"

My therapist gave me the assignment to dig below "unfavorable" feelings to find the buried unmet need(s). As humans, we all have basic needs. Below is a list of some of them and where I stand on each.

Safety, Security, Survival

My parents effectively met my basic needs of safety, security, and survival. I was fed when hungry, had a roof over my head, was dressed appropriately for the weather, was taken to the doctor when ill, and was physically safe. I had the fundamental necessities to thrive.

Touch

All humans crave affection. We are social beings, and healthy touch is necessary for emotional growth and development.

As a child, I didn't get cuddled often. I was kissed goodnight by my mom and told to have pleasant dreams, a routine I've continued with my kids.

If I was sad, I cried in my room. To this day, I bury my face in my sleeve or turn away when teary-eyed. Maybe it's about fearing a loss of control in front of others, the same as it is with anger.

I am affectionate with my husband and children. I don't mind loving touch when I'm in a good mood.

My husband is cuddly when I'm sad, and I feel soothed by it.

Attention

Receiving attention makes us feel valued. As infants, we need attention to meet our basic security, survival, and safety needs.

Growing up, I received more negative attention from my father than loving care. That came during his later years.

I craved attention from my mother. I wanted to be a priority over work but rarely felt I was. I learned early on I could receive more attention by being sick. Similar to my father's attention, it was negative, but something was better than nothing. When I sang, my mom gave me admiration and praise, which encouraged me to do it often.

Feeling heard is the type of attention I seek the most—without feedback, advice, criticism, or judgment.

Underlying Message: Being sick brought me attention, albeit negative.

Mirroring

Mirroring involves reflecting an emotion. It can include facial expressions, body posture, and other sounds and movements, which validate another person.

Receiving heavy sighs, lack of eye contact and receptive attention, and getting interrupted sent the message that what I had to say wasn't important or valued and was bothersome.

Guidance

Guidance involves receiving advice and help, as well as modeling appropriate social skills from our caregivers.

Hearing my father scream at employees at the family business was awful. There's no other way to describe it. Fortunately, I learned how *not* to behave. Speaking critically and harshly to others was something I never wanted to emulate because I saw how it affected the recipients of his wrath, myself included.

Most advice I sought was given by my sisters, mostly about boys and such. My mom was overly conservative when it came to the topic of sex. A lot of her guidance in that area taught me to fear trusting men.

Secrets.

We had so many family secrets. Shame was the underlying theme to them. With that shame came a fear of outsiders judging and being unaccepting. Hence, I keep my feelings a secret unless they are happy ones. It's what my parents taught me was appropriate.

I think I was well-behaved to avoid drama or getting into trouble. I was the "perfect" child.

My role models were an alcoholic with little patience and a workaholic who missed precious moments.

I guided myself to do the right thing.

What I did learn from my parents was loyalty and sticking together through thick and thin. That's something I've carried with me into my marriage. Communication is essential.

Listening and Acceptance

Being heard and accepted involves getting respect and having our feelings validated and tolerated.

That often wasn't the case in my home. I wasn't insulted or degraded for being who I am, but there was a lack of tolerance for my opinions.

When it came to sharing about home issues, my mom took the conversations as a personal attack. Instead of taking responsibility for her actions, I received guilt.

Underlying Message: Don't share because nothing will change, and you'll end up feeling miserable.

Grieve Losses

Grieving or grief is a natural response to loss—when something or someone we care for is taken away from us.

I gave myself time to grieve the loss of my dad. There have been intermittent and out-of-the-blue bouts of sadness, as well. I allow myself to experience them.

With the breakup of my first love, the pain was devasting. It led me to fear getting into another relationship because I never wanted to experience such heartache again. It was brutal. God bless my husband for sticking by me during those early months when I kept trying to push him away.

Support

Lack of emotional support can leave us feeling alone and lonely. We have an innate need to connect with others.

I've taken classes for self-growth and have been in therapy since college. Yet, I often feel left on my own without emotional support, something I do to myself. I don't reach out because I don't want to burden others and don't feel emotionally safe. I also don't want to be judged or belittled.

Often when I share at home, I get psychoanalyzed, which makes me clam up. I don't consider that type of support safe. It is a form of unintentional judgment because my mistakes are pointed out, the errors of my ways.

Today, I ask to be heard and not for advice when I don't want it. Sure, there are occasions when I like feedback, but sometimes, I just want to dump what's on my mind.

Loyalty and Trust

Loyalty refers to receiving support, devotion, and faithfulness from another person, whereas trust refers to relying on someone's ability, character, truth, or strength and having confidence in them.

To me, loyalty and trust are a two-way street, a give and take. Unfortunately, friendships have repeatedly taught me how to distrust others. They've been primarily one-sided.

Betrayal by women has led me to avoid getting close to many. It is this need where I'm often alone, isolated, and afraid to reach out. The underlying fear is rejection.

Underlying Message: Constant rejections lead to the belief I'm not important enough for someone to give me their unconditional friendship.

Achievement

Accomplishing what we set our minds out to do brings confidence.

Having a mother who did everything for me didn't allow me to take many risks while growing up, which resulted in me missing numerous opportunities to gain a sense of independence.

Regarding my daily activities, I am an over-achiever.

Where I under-achieve is with the core belief that I'm competent and independent even though I consistently prove otherwise. It's no surprise to me, coming from the do-everything-for-me guidance I received as a youth.

Fun and Inner Fulfillment

When we fulfill our needs in all aspects of our lives, i.e., work, relationships, and bask in the simple pleasures life has to offer, we gain happiness and inner fulfillment.

I am spontaneous with my kids and have fun. We do many activities together and are creating beautiful memories.

While growing up, most of the fun I had was with my sisters and friends. There wasn't much quality "family time." For the most part, each person did their own thing. I sang in my room, did creative writing, and used other creative outlets to express and entertain myself.

I often lack the desire to try something new. I'm a creature of habit. There is security in knowing what to expect without surprises, which boils down to control.

Developing my sense of spirituality is something I do for myself that fills and brightens my inner light.

Creative writing and seeing my novels available to the public brings an enormous sense of inner fulfillment, as does watching my children develop and thrive.

Sexuality

Sexuality as a need doesn't just refer to intercourse. It involves feeling comfortable in our skin and discovering our likes and dislikes as sexual beings.

I accept myself as a sexual woman. Having trust in my husband has made it easier for me to experiment and feel safe.

As a young adult, the messages I received from my mother made me fear men. My first kiss was during my junior year of high school. My first sexual relationship came during college with my first boyfriend, who waited months until I was ready to move forward intimately. He was a patient soul. It worked to my benefit and made me feel secure and prepared to take that next step in our relationship.

Freedom

We need to take risks, be spontaneous, and explore our interests while also taking personal responsibility for our actions.

I pause when I feel impulsive, especially when it comes to making big decisions. My husband and I have an agreement to wait twenty-four hours when the decision involves something huge.

I feel free to explore my interests, write in my genre, and do activities I enjoy. I don't need permission from anyone to do so, either. Having this freedom brings a sense of satisfaction.

Nurturing and Attachment

Being nurtured is critical for healthy social and intellectual growth. When we have healthy attachments to our caregivers and feel cared for, we develop trust.

I view this need as another two-way street, similar to loyalty and trust. We must not only nurture but be nurtured as well, as both kids *and* adults.

Regarding attachment, my fear of my father in early childhood created an unhealthy attachment to my mother, which led to codependency and the false belief that I can't do things on my own.

I often close myself off from receiving emotional and physical nourishment. It goes back to touch. I'm uncomfortable receiving it in the form of affection when I'm sad unless it's from my husband.

I'm an empath, so naturally, I try to support those in need, usually in the form of listening with compassionate ears.

Opening myself up and being vulnerable feels unsafe. My body screams, "Leave me alone!" while my heart screams for connection and acceptance.

Unconditional Love

Unconditional love involves giving or receiving love without expectations. It provides a sense of security and acceptance.

I believe that loving and receiving love without conditions is hard to come by, especially when it involves loving ourselves.

My sister wants nothing to do with me. She is a blood relative. Friends claimed they would stick by me, only to ditch me. That isn't unconditional love. It is a lack of communication.

After being in my husband's life for twenty-eight years and counting, I still question whether he will continue to love me unconditionally. The reality is he hasn't left yet and affirms his love daily. My insecurity in this area is a result of many life experiences.

Underlying Message: I am not worthy enough to work through kinks that arise. Instead, cease all interactions.

Your Turn

This section is a doozy. Go through each need and see how it fits into your life.

What needs were never met?

What needs were met with ease?

Which needs require(d) more attention?

After exploring the various needs, do any underlying messages pop out as they did for me?

This might be another entry to work on with a professional. A lot of discoveries came out of this assignment. My therapist and I refer back to it often when I'm struggling. It's usually because a need is being unmet.

No Escape: Smothered

My Turn

My list of things to do is suffocating: laundry, caretaking, work, bills, my mom's emotional well-being—hello, codependency—and so on.

There have also been ongoing health issues at home, thankfully, not related to COVID.

The childhood messages I received were:

"I'll take care of it for you."

"I'll call and straighten it out."

"It's too much for you."

My mother fed me these lines repeatedly. They have become deeply-rooted in my soul and set me up for failure, even with my successes.

When I was agoraphobic for six weeks and wouldn't leave home, not one sister called me. Not one sorority sister checked in with me. My mom never took off work unless it was to take me for a medical test to see why I had vertigo for so many weeks (anxiety).

My mother reinforced my agoraphobia by enabling me to remain housebound. Today I know she wasn't aware of the condition and didn't understand it. Neither did I.

Leaving my last semester of undergrad because of paralyzing anxiety gave me feelings of failure, inadequacy, and incapability.

Experience has proven that my mother's words, both directly and indirectly through behaviors, were correct.

I'm trying to rewire my brain with new messages. It takes practice and conscious effort. The old tapes sneak in and tell me everything is too much. It angers me that I have to prove that bullshit wrong. I am more than capable. Life has demonstrated that.

Fifty years of doubt won't disappear overnight. This work is ongoing, but I see a difference and, more importantly, *feel* the difference. It's incredible to pat myself on the back for a job well done. The past never allowed me to do that.

Your Turn

Do you ever feel there's no escape from the old tapes that play in your head, tapes recorded by other people's viewpoints?

Do you feel there's no escape from self-doubt?

What would it take to change that?

What is one thing you can do to prove to yourself you are capable?

Perfection doesn't qualify. Expectations must be reasonable. I'm referring to making a conscious effort and patting yourself on the back for *trying*.

When I was agoraphobic, I didn't magically start going to crowded places. It began with standing on my driveway—a massive undertaking at the time. It progressed to walking to the mailbox across the street.

There were setbacks. I'd have panic attacks and want to retreat to the safety of my house. The key was I would attempt an outing again, big or small, and praise myself for trying.

This type of exposure was my way out. Am I free from panic attacks? No. But I no longer run from them. I have enough tools to walk through them.

It's the same with ED. With small exposures, whether it's trying a new food until we're not affected by eating it or changing one thing about our behavior, confidence slowly builds. ED hates when we feel confident. It wants us to remain fragile and weak.

Helplessness is a state of mind. I know this sounds cruel, but it's so true.

Life is hard.

Change is hard.

There is an escape. It involves making changes.

With this in mind, what is one healthy change you can make to prove a self-defeating thought wrong?

It doesn't have to be gigantic—every change for the better counts.

What About Me?

My Turn

Many days I feel lost in the crowd while those important to me take center stage. They have all eyes on them, receive praise, encouragement, and an abundance of attention.

Wow, how cool would it be to stand next to them instead of being alone in the audience?

I give and give until there's nothing left. Not even for myself. The outcome is exhaustion. It's an ongoing theme in my life.

There is only so much energy one can exert without refueling. Each day is like an Olympic trial. I give it my all and go overboard. The cost is a depletion of self. I then ask, "What about me? Don't I deserve as much as the next person?"

The answer is yes. The kicker is I have to feel worthy of another person's love and attention and have to ask for what I need.

My husband makes it known when he wants to spend more time with me.

My kids let me know when they need me.

ED lets me know I'm incompetent if I can't please everyone and make them happy.

The dogs let me know when they're hungry or want to go outside.

My stomach doesn't tell me I'm hungry until the point of starvation. My hunger cues aren't as effective as they should be, which is why I eat on a timed schedule, regardless of whether I'm hungry or not, to prevent drops in my blood sugar.

My thoughts tell me to add one more thing to my chore list even though my body is screaming for a break.

My head aches from working on the computer for hours on end, but I know I can edit one more chapter or reconcile one more account.

Guilt tells me I'm not doing enough, period. The house *should* be neater. Dinner *should* be on the table. Clothes *should* be folded once dry. The bed *should* be made in the morning. The dishes *should* be loaded into the dishwasher or washed. The bills *should* be paid today even though they aren't due yet.

Should.

Should.

Should.

Do I tell my kids they should do a million tasks in a day?

NO.

Then why do I expect it from myself?

It goes back to the core belief of feeling incapable. To counteract this belief, I overdo it, which leads to anxiety, overwhelm, and tiredness. The physical symptoms that result reinforce my original assumption that I'm incapable. I mean, if I were competent, wouldn't I be able to effectively handle the tasks I assign myself without so many adverse aftereffects?

The statement that stands out to me the most from the above paragraph is, "The tasks I assign myself."

I am the only one who puts undue pressure on myself to perform.

Does the cost outweigh the benefit?

The sad reality is it doesn't. The detriment to my mental and physical health causes the overwhelm to seep into all other aspects of my life. It isn't fair to anyone, especially me.

Your Turn

Do you feel you are more of a giver or a receiver?

What is the benefit of your choice?

What is the pitfall?

Do you verbalize your needs to others? Why? Why not?

What would it take for you to do so?

With whom do you feel safe enough to express your needs?

What are your expectations about getting them met?

Are your requests of others feasible?

Do you think others should know what you need even if you haven't vocalized it?

How does that affect your relationships with those people?

How can you let others know they haven't respectably met your needs?

Do you put an excessive amount of pressure on yourself to perform?

Do you consider yourself a perfectionist?

What would happen if you weren't perfect?

How would you view yourself?

How do you think others would perceive you?

Are you putting undue pressure on yourself to be perfect, or is it coming from someone else?

No matter who it comes from, do you think it's fair to expect perfection when it doesn't exist?

I will repeat, perfection *does not* exist.

Allow this to sink in.

How can you ease up on yourself?

Not everything is an emergency. Define what constitutes immediate attention versus what can wait to erase some of the shoulds on your Right Now list.

Tea For One

My Turn

My therapist asked me to explore my heightened anxiety about my mom's aging. As I've discussed in previous entries, it's as if I'm grieving a loss that hasn't transpired yet.

In a sense, it's a protective mechanism. If I emotionally pull back, then when "that day" finally arrives, it will be less traumatic.

That false belief is a crock of shit. All the preparation in the world won't prevent grief from the loss of a loved one.

I think back to my earlier years and don't recall many fun memories of us doing things together, other than my singing to her or performing in shows.

I've created many shared experiences with my children to save them from suffering the loss and abandonment I felt.

The following is a poem I wrote that gets to the nitty-gritty of what resides in my heart when it comes to my mother. As with everything I encounter, I see both good and bad. This poem is no different.

We never had a tea party,
I can't remember us playing with dolls.
I played teacher with my stuffed animals,
Round people were a ball.

Where were you?

I failed at taking my driver's test,
I wanted you to bring me there again.
You sent the housekeeper to do your job,
The thrill lost its allure. You weren't there to cheer for me in the end.

Where were you?

TV in the family room,
You were always on the phone.
Dinner conversations were unstimulating,
I may as well have eaten alone.

You were present when I sang,
And when I performed on a stage.
You brought me to singing lessons,
And have been my number one fan in writing every page.

The solution to friend troubles,
Was to go shopping for new clothes.
Better hide our bags in the closet, though,
To keep dad in the dark, so he never knows.

No chaperoning on a field trip,
No movies, at least not with you.
No help with homework when I struggled,
Others watched me through mono, strep throat, and the flu.

Years later, the dance steps repeated,
Work was the excuse you gave.
Missed time with the grandkids, mostly me,
The pain in my heart was additive. Your attention was what I craved.

Your weekly doctor visits,
Scared me to no end.
If something happened to you,
On whom would I depend?

Sickness gave you attention,
That you craved for sympathy.
All it did was fill me with worry,
And shield you from your misery.

Did you ever love my father?
I do believe you did.
Loved but never in love,
Since the time I was a kid.

You were my only protector,
Tried to shield me from the stress.
Kept secrets, would never tell me,
Which created anxiety, panic, and distress.

If I'm not capable of handling life,
The message I was sent.
Then when it throws me curveballs,
They're met with torment and discontent.

Yet through it all you were my constant,
Always there without a doubt.
Cheering, praising, a listening ear,
Unconditional love throughout.

So here I stand at a crossroad,
Full of love but anger too.
Fear of how the world will look,
When I no longer have you.

Work was your addiction,
Dad's was alcohol.
My sister had her drugs,
I was scared of substances and hated them all.

I am sad you missed out on so much,
In that respect, we don't see eye to eye.
Making time to be present with my kids,
Has been a conscious effort to supply.

My heart hurts from missing you,
For all the times you said you can't.
For making excuses that there will be a next time,
For which you would rarely grant.

My kids are privileged to see a side of you,
I missed out on because you were too busy.
Having lunch dates, calls, and visits,
Enjoying quality time chatting or watching TV.

As time drifts by I notice,
I keep active during the time we share.
I'm either cleaning, watching something, or busying myself,
To distract me because my sad feelings are too hard to bear.

As a result, guilt eats at me,
Because I should make the best of our time spent.
But emotionally I pull away,
A barrier to protect myself, this mechanism buried in cement.

I am sad for the time we lost out on,
The fun we could have had.
But thankful for what you were capable of giving,
Not all the memories are bad.

Laughing in hysterics,
Sharing Mommy, Mommy jokes 'til you cried.
Squeezing food between my teeth,
Giggling about old times until we were teary-eyed.

It's been a mix of happy/sad,
Life is filled with ups and downs.
Through it all, I'm grateful to have had you as a mom,
Because when it came to acceptance, love, and support, you indeed wore the crown.

I am blessed to have a mother who loves me unconditionally and is always there when I need a listening ear. I can look back and say she did the best she could to raise five daughters while running a successful business with an alcoholic husband who entered recovery. I admire her dedication to her children and husband. She cared for my father until his dying day, showing him only love and support. The qualities of loyalty, commitment, trust, and nonjudgment are what I bring into my relationships with my children and husband.

Your Turn

We all have baggage we carry from our past. Who do you feel handed you the most that you still hold on to?

If there has been sexual or physical abuse, this would be a topic to work on with a trusted professional because traumatic feelings might arise and be triggered when exploring these ideas.

Do you see any positive outcomes that resulted from those relationships?

I can say my father taught me a great deal about the importance of being a spiritual person. He lived a spiritual life after joining AA. I admired his strength, altruistic nature, and courage to face trying situations because of his faith in a Higher Power. I have come to believe in my own over the years. My faith in it strengthens the more I see it work in my life.

Do you put up barriers when it comes to dealing with certain people?

Sadly, I put them up when I'm around my mom, who I know loves me dearly. It has become an instinct when I'm around her. I have patience with her, listen to her stories, and advise when needed. Affection is the area where I have trouble. It was the same with my father. Whenever there was affection, I felt cringy. It wasn't until his last year of life that I could hug him with pure love. I want to get to that point with my mom and am working on tearing down the walls.

Is there anyone you wish you could tear down the walls for?

What would happen if you did?

For me, I think sadness would reach a breaking point because I'm so afraid to lose my mother. Isn't it ironic how I hold back from demonstrative affection toward her yet crave her love and attention? It's fascinating how the psyche works to protect us as children and how those same mechanisms carry over into adulthood.

Do you recognize how the methods used to cope with individual family members carried into adulthood, even when those people are no longer a threat or hold power over you?

Nobody has power over us as adults unless we give it to them. To me, seizing our power back is a boot camp experience to put into practice. It comes down to setting boundaries and speaking up for ourselves.

How can you take your power back from someone who is trying to control you?

It's yours and yours alone.

****

Add on during editing.

I am happy to say I have come to a place of complete love and acceptance for my mother, with no residual anger or blame. It is beyond freeing to be in this space, the same as it was with my father. When she and I are together, I can *be* with her, enjoy the precious moments, and create fond new memories. It took hard work but has been well worth it.

Section XI
Wrapping It Up... This Time I Mean It

I wish I could tell you ED has left the building and vanished into thin air. Unfortunately, that's not the case, which goes back to my belief in *recovering* versus *recovered*.

I am traveling on a path without a finish line, in constant motion, learning more about myself in the process. There is a sense of freedom with this outlook. For those who have fully recovered, I commend you.

What I have gained over my years in recovery is knowledge. I'm aware of ED's voice and can clearly distinguish it from my healthy voice. This clarity enables me to get up faster when I fall.

When I entered my first round of treatment, I was half-in, half-out. I was scared for my life, but not to the point of fully surrendering to recovery.

I remember the nutritionist setting a goal weight, and I thought she was out of her mind. ED agreed. My body distortion was off the charts.

My glasses are more transparent today. I'm at the goal weight initially set and am content with it. Of course, when my therapist tells me she'd like the number to go higher, ED steps in and says, "Excuse me?"

With a better perspective comes the reality of how sick I was before entering treatment for ED—both times.

In my earlier days, my attitude was, "I'll get help if the number on the scale dips below so and so."

The reality is, at some point, it's too late. Look what happened to Sleeping Beauty. I'm grateful it wasn't too late for me.

In an earlier entry, I said I never wanted to go back to treatment. Well, I did. I'm imperfect and allowed to make mistakes. Hell, I make them every day. And guess what? The world hasn't ended.

My journey has given me more than I could have ever asked for. It's given me ME! I'm on the PhD road to self-discovery, and it feels fantastic. I would never have acquired such a deep sense of self if I hadn't reached my breaking point and sought help.

My outlook is more positive. My patience has grown with myself and others. Things aren't as black and white as they used to be. I can see in color now, which is much more gratifying and fulfilling.

Yes, ED still wins occasionally. However, my fear of where it can take me is the strongest it has ever been. That, to me, is significant growth. I must remain aware of ED's ultimate plan. I'm not ready to give up on life yet. I have too much to live for. I hope you do too!

Here's to the love and light in all of us.

Romance Titles
Faith Starr

I am taking a risk by sharing my pen name for my romance novels with my Faith Elicia readers. I don't let the two overlap, mainly to protect the confidentiality of my family. If you choose to read them and post reviews or share publicly, I ask that there be no reference to Faith Elicia. I never mention Faith Elicia in anything Faith Starr related. I thank you in advance for respecting my wishes.

Faith Starr's books are all standalones but are best read in sequence. They are all available on Amazon and in the Kindle Unlimited library.

The HILLTOPS Series
Destiny
Purity
Diversity

The MUSIC FOR THE HEART Series
Hold Me
Promise to Fulfill
Risk Worth Taking
Remember Me
The Right Time
Holding Out

Novellas
Sinful Agreement

For more information about upcoming releases, please visit
https://www.faithstarr.com/

Follow Faith Starr Books on social media

Pinterest (A true Pinterest junkie)
https://www.pinterest.com/FaithStarrBooks/

Instagram
https://www.instagram.com/faithstarrbooks/?hl=en

Facebook
https://www.facebook.com/FaithStarrBooks/

About Faith Elicia

There's not much to add since I've already shared my story. So here's some info about my alter ego, Faith Starr.

When I'm not managing my husband's medical practice or handling things for one of my three kids—both of which take up an enormous amount of time—I escape to the confines of my home office to write romance fiction, my passion.

There is absolutely nothing like creating fictional characters, getting into their minds, and giving them a life of their own with all the emotions that go along with it. I am swept away, head over heels in love, with each alpha male I create and the confident women who steal their hearts. These characters have become a part of me that will live on forever.

Being a romantic at heart, with a bit of a dirty mind, I relish creating believable stories that touch upon readers' heartstrings, provoke thought, and hopefully provide a bit of insight into some heavy topics.

Being married for over twenty-six years—holy cow, how time flies—I am a firm believer in the concept of "Once Upon a Time" and "Happily Ever After" because I have found mine. Aww, I know, so mushy. But that's me in a nutshell, a softie with a big heart, just like my characters! A bit of a nut too.

Website
Faithelicia.com

Follow Faith Elicia on social media

Facebook
https://www.facebook.com/Faith-Elicia-103771477901583/

Instagram
https://www.instagram.com/faitheliciag/?hl=en

Please Review My Book

Book reviews mean a lot to an author. If you have a minute or two, I'd appreciate it if you could please provide an honest, sincere review.

Thanks so much, Faith

Musical Inspiration

Twenty-One Pilots

A shout-out to my daughter, who introduced me to Twenty-One Pilots! They have become my go-to whenever I'm down. Their older work is raw and emotional. It makes me feel a part of instead of separate from.

The songs that affect me the most are:

"Before You Start Your Day"
"Friend, Please"
"Truce"
"Trees"
"Kitchen Sink" (This one has worn out my speakers)

Katy Perry
"Pearl"

This song is incredible. If I'm reading into the lyrics correctly, they refer to an abusive partner. Building on that train of thought, I let ED represent the abuser, and the song took on an entirely new meaning. It's both empowering and enlightening.

Natalie Cole
"Starting Over Again"

When I went to treatment for agoraphobia, this song became my anthem. The beautiful and late Natalie Cole sings about a relationship. I switched the message and made it about me starting over, moving on, and moving forward.

Selena Gomez
"Who Says?"
"Live Like There's No Tomorrow" (This one brings me into the moment. It's both inspiring and uplifting.)
"Stars Dance"
"Anxiety" (Julia Michaels ft. Selena Gomez)

I originally bought my daughter a Selena Gomez CD as a gift years ago and loved it so much that I kept it. I have since been a huge fan of her music. So passionate. Love her.

Madonna
"Oh, Father"

I sang this song often in my youth to help me deal with the anger I felt toward my father.

Christina Aguilera
"Hurt"
"Reflection"

Jody Watley
"It All Begins With You"

A spiritual gem!

Clay Aiken
"I Will Carry You"
"Shine"

Back Street Boys
"Larger Than Life"

Avril Lavigne
"Head Above Water"

Help And Support Are Available

Alliance For Eating Disorder Awareness
The Alliance is a national non-profit organization dedicated to education, early intervention, outreach, support, and advocacy for all eating disorders. The website provides an abundance of relevant information and resources for individuals who suffer from eating disorders. The Alliance can suggest professionals in the eating disorder field along with treatment options. It is an invaluable resource.
https://www.allianceforeatingdisorders.com/

Healthy Place
Healthyplace.com is the largest consumer mental health site online. They provide authoritative information and support to people with mental health concerns, along with their family members and other loved ones.
https://www.healthyplace.com/eating-disorders

National Association of Anorexia Nervosa and Associated Disorders
ANAD is the leading nonprofit in the U.S. that provides free peer support services to anyone struggling with an eating disorder, regardless of age, race, gender identity, sexual orientation, or background. Their nationwide network of volunteers understand first-hand the ups and downs of the recovery journey—because they, too, have lived the experience of an eating disorder. ANAD empowers volunteers to help others through their own recovery.
https://anad.org/

National Eating Disorder Association
The National Eating Disorders Association (NEDA) is the largest nonprofit organization dedicated to supporting individuals and families affected by eating disorders. NEDA serves as a catalyst for prevention, cures, and quality care access.
https://www.nationaleatingdisorders.org/

Overeaters Anonymous
Overeaters Anonymous (OA) is a community of people who support each other in order to recover from compulsive eating and food behaviors. They welcome anyone who feels they have a problem with food. It is a Twelve-Step Program.
https://oa.org/

Courses:
Mindfulness-Based Stress-Reduction
Below is the link for the 8-Week Mindfulness-Based Stress-Reduction Course. It is FREE online. This was how I took the program. Some cities provide it live for a fee. There are many lectures on YouTube that explore some of the practices. Amazing course!
https://palousemindfulness.com/MBSR/week0.html

Mindful Self-Compassion
Below is the link for the 8-Week Mindful Self-Compassion Course. This class has a fee. It is offered live and online. I took it via Zoom. There are many speakers on YouTube who teach some of the practices.
https://self-compassion.org/the-program/

Foreword Provided By:
Benaaz Russell, PsyD, CEDS
Former Director of Admissions of Monte Nido and Affiliates and Clinical Director of Casa Verde at Oliver-Pyatt Centers, former Program Director at The Lukens Institute, former primary therapist and IOP team leader at The Renfrew Center, former primary therapist at The Watershed, former primary therapist at The Palm Beach Institute's Eating Disorder Center
https://www.wellingtonbehavioralhealth.com/

Stephanie Klein, RD, LDN, RYT
Former dietitian for Center For Discovery – Eating Disorder Treatment Center, West Palm Beach, Florida
https://dessertsoverdiets.com/

Acknowledgments

A big thank you to all the supportive individuals who have guided me along my journey thus far.

Thank you, Valentin Sora at Sceneticdesigns.com, for the interior layout, design, picture organization, cover, and keen attention to detail. I'm so appreciative of the editor's cap you put on during the back and forth process. Your patience is unsurpassed. I couldn't have asked for a better designer to assist with this project. My sincere gratitude for putting it all together and making the workbook shine.

Hugs and kisses to the girls in my CODA group. You have stuck by me during my ups and downs, and I am ever so grateful for your acceptance, love, and continued support.

A gratitude hug goes to Sherry, the Art Therapist who inspired this entire project. It began with a drawing, and then another. Add journal entries, and voilà, this workbook was born. Thank you so much for encouraging individuality and allowing my markers to bring my feelings to light.

A hug goes to the facilitators and women at the Alliance for Eating Disorder Awareness for always being there with open arms. You have played an instrumental role in my recovery. I want to personally thank Lorraine Mari, PhD, and Johanna Kandel for being supportive all these years and making recommendations for treatment, therapists, and dietitians.

A special thank you to Dr. Finder. I may be a blip on your radar, but you will forever be in my heart for kicking my butt into gear and onto the road of recovery.

Jeanette Dipento, LCSW. I want to acknowledge you for being by my side for so many years. We may no longer have a professional relationship, but you taught me many valuable strategies and tools that I use to this day, and for that, I thank you.

A warm thank you goes to Stephanie Klein, LDN, RD, RYT, for being such a lovable dietitian. I'm grateful to have you as part of my team and for all of your encouragement and support. You are a doll. I appreciate your contribution to the Foreword and value you as a person. You're a sweetie.

A squeezable hug goes to Benaaz Russell, PsyD, CEDS, for being such an influential part of my journey. Your insight astounds me. You push me harder than I want to go but with a gentle shove—not literally, of course. Your happy dances make me smile, your sporadic texts make my days, and your faith in me heightens my own. I am so blessed to have you in my life, a person I can share everything with. Thank you for your contribution to the Foreword and your ongoing support during the tedious editing stages when I complained nonstop and wanted to give up.

What can I say to my children? You are the most precious beings on the planet to me. Your unconditional love inspires me every day. I receive it in your support, encouragement, and excitement for all I do to better myself. I hope my discoveries have made me a better listener, a more present mother, and most importantly, a positive role model for setting your mind to something and following through with it. We can, and we will! I love you with all my heart.

My husband deserves a million thank-yous for remaining on this roller coaster with me. You've seen me at my best and my worst and love me through it all. The love that fills my heart has no boundaries when it comes to you. Thank you for giving me space to do my thing and follow my path. I am ever so grateful for your loyalty, dedication, and continuous support. As we've said since the beginning, "It's always an adventure." This undertaking is yet another one. Here's to many more in the years to come.

I am eternally grateful to have a mother who has always stood by my side with no judgment. You are and always will be my biggest cheerleader. I love you forever and with all my heart. I am so blessed to have such a devoted mom.

A big thank you goes to my father. You deserve recognition for inspiring me to put my pride aside and be of service to others. I only share my truth to give a complete picture of my story, not to throw blame. You were a loving father with a heart of gold. Your later years are cherished the most because I saw firsthand the kind person you were. I hope you are looking down and smiling with the knowledge that I am continuing your legacy of helping others. I love you above and beyond and miss you every day.

Finally, I am grateful to my Higher Power for being my guiding light. Thank you for giving me the courage to face another day, the strength to get through it, and the faith that all will be well. With love in my heart, gifted by you, I dare to publish this book. Through gritted teeth, I am putting myself out there for all to see. The freedom comes from knowing you are holding my hand.

Workbook Copyrights

Above The Line entry – Top 20 Training (Top 20 Press) www.top20training.com

Goo Gone manufactured by Weiman Products, LLC

Audrey & ED entry – Ted plush inspired by *Ted*, the live-action/CG-animated film from Family Guy creator Seth MacFarlane

Christian Grey entry – Inspired by the *Fifty Shades Trilogy* written by E.L. James

Cookie Jar entry – Inspired by *Who Stole The Cookies From The Cookie Jar* nursery rhyme – public domain in law, as specified on Amazon

Drama In Your Life entry – Inspired by:
Annie (Original 1982 Motion Picture Soundtrack) – Sony Legacy
Chicago: Music From the Motion Picture – Sony Legacy
Rock of Ages (Original Broadway Cast Recording) – Watertower Music
Wicked (2003 Original Broadway Cast) – Verve

Gray Skies entry – Inspired by the song "Put On A Happy Face" – Music by Charles Strouse, Lyrics by Lee Adams

In A Fix entry – "Felix The Cat" theme song written by Winston Sharples

I Think I Can entry – Inspired by *The Little Engine That Could (Original Classic Edition)* by Watty Piper. Author: George Hauman Illustrators: George Hauman, Doris Hauman. July 31, 2001 Edition

It's Always The Same entry – Barney the Dinosaur created by Sheryl Lyna Stamps-Leach

Just Go To Sleep entry – Thomas The Tank Engine created by Reverend Wilbert Awdry

Let's Make A Deal entry – *Let's Make A Deal* created and produced by Stefan Hatos and Monty Hall

Magnified entry – Illustration inspired by the book *The Ants Go Marching One By One* Paperback – January 1, 1999 – Scholastic Version by n/a (Author), Richard Bernal (Illustrator)

Posse Of One entry – Sybil based on book by Flora Rheta Schreiber. Movie (1976) Lorimar Productions. Screenplay by Stewart Stern

Seesaw Of Needs entry – Hierarchy of Human Needs packet provided by Benaaz Russell, PsyD, CEDS. We were unable to identify the source, as it is dated. The only information listed on the packet is "20 – Human Needs." The information presented has been revised and adapted from the original material.

The Show Must Go On entry – "The Show Must Go On" written by Brian May; "Bohemian Rhapsody" written by Freddie Mercury

Time To Walk entry – Inspired by *Saturday Night Fever – The Original Movie Soundtrack* – RSO Records, Polydor, Reprise

To Eat Or Not To Eat entry – "To be, or not to be" – Shakespeare's Hamlet

What's Inside The Windows entry – Sully and Mike Wazowski. Monsters, Inc. produced by Pixar Animation Studios and distributed by Walt Disney Pictures

Where In The World Is Matt Lauer entry – Where In The World Is Matt Lauer – NBC's *Today* Segment

www.ingramcontent.com/pod-product-compliance
Lightning Source LLC
Chambersburg PA
CBHW051802100526
44592CB00016B/2530